The Big Little School

The Big
Little School

SUNDAY CHILD OF AMERICAN PROTESTANTISM

by Robert W. Lynn *and* Elliott Wright

HARPER & ROW, Publishers

New York, Evanston, San Francisco, London

1817

For Luther A. Weigle

CONTENTS

"Give Me that Old-Time" School: 1910-1945
Orthodoxy Meets Neo-Orthodoxy (1945–)
It Just Keeps Rolling Along

Reaching for "Lost Beginnings"

The past will have to be examined in regard to its own future. All history is full of possibilities— possibilities that have been profited by . . ., seized and blocked. In this perspective it appears full of interrupted possibilities, lost beginnings, arrested onsets upon the future.

—JÜRGEN MOLTMANN[1]

The road from Maryville to Knoxville runs north for twenty miles through the virtually flat triangle of bottomland formed as the Tennessee and Little Tennessee Rivers come together. South of Mt. Olive and beyond Fort Loudon Lake, the Blue Ridge foothills jut up as the larger stream comes into view. Around some bends and over a bridge is Knoxville, where dogwood-shaded avenues spiral out from a business district perched on a cliff. Before the young Sam Keen was able to follow that route, he knew another road better—the one from Damascus to Jerusalem. He had never been on that faraway thoroughfare, or in the Judean countryside which he learned earlier than the topography of Tennessee. But he knew that Jesus loved him and would walk with him when he was old enough to get around the state.[2]

Sam Keen the adult—theologian and cogent commentator on America's society and psyche—vividly remembered which geography he knew first and why: the Protestant Sunday school. His experience in Maryville is hardly unique. Millions have memorized the map of the Holy Land before they could get out of home towns. The Sunday school as movement and institution has made an indelible mark on the entire cultural and educational experience of American Protestant generations. But the collective and historical memory of what the Sunday school has done is today generally hazy, clouded by an image of Sunday instruction as a sentimental relic. The dynamics which etched a picture of a Middle-Eastern road in Sam Keen's mind have been and are at work in the United States. For the sake of a nation's understanding of itself, the Sunday school heritage and its lingering influence must be unclouded.

A limited awareness of the guts and marrow of history, while not indigenously American, does prevail throughout the Republic. Presentations of the past are characteristically political, often superficial, and frequently military in outline. The story moves from Indian entanglements to the Revolution, through the Civil War and conflict on the western range, to world wars, then —with a pause for Korea—to Indo-China. The culture-making interaction of ideologies, movements, and nonpolitical institutions seldom comes into the picture except at the edges. The study of popular religion is neglected by the churches as well as by secular scholars. Yet popular religion is reflected in the everyday attitudes and beliefs of vast numbers of people. It may not be the *best* expression of faith or have official ecclesiastical sanction or agree with academic theology—but it is an apt cultural mirror. Popular religion has emotions; its songs and history make for good storytelling.

The best example, indeed the epitome, of popular American Protestantism is the Sunday school, perhaps as old as the nation and part of the stuff of history. Particularly forceful in molding America between the War of 1812 and World War I, the institution is vastly more important than is probably realized by its modern supporters or depreciators or by those non-Protestants who are relatively unaware of its present or earlier forms. In a day when every segment of society is inundated with crises, the need to know how and what shaped the inherited culture is crucial. Any present is linked to the past by obvious or hidden continuities; any future will by affected by the way those continuities are understood and transmitted.

Sunday school history reveals much about America's hidden continuities with the past—hidden partly because the present-day institution is but an echo of what it once was. Even though biblical geography and songs like "Jesus Loves Me" remain essential in conservative and sectarian Protestant classrooms, and routine in those of many middle-class mainline churches, the zeal for them has waned. The fact that the fire is banked, and may or may not again be given fresh fuel, in no way lessens the continuing influence of an energetic history.

Succinctly put, the Sunday school is American Protestantism's training ground. Denominations have established hundreds of colleges and universities, but the Sunday school is the *big* school in matters religious for the Protestant people—originally and especially white people, though it has played a distinctive role in the religious experience and culture of black America. Compared to public education, Sunday school is marginal to American society, yet is an important *little* school in the rearing of the whole nation. The Sunday school is the big little school of the United States.

It is not mere accident that the average citizen is unaware of the institution's far-reaching influence, even if he could trace the road from Damascus to Jerusalem at an early age. For fifty years a hefty and vocal segment of the Protestant forces has preached and predicted its demise, accused the Sunday classes of weakness and excessive gentility, and proposed alternatives for Christian education. The mood of Sunday schools may be an affront to the more rigorous education encouraged by universities. A Sunday school mentality may explain why American Protestant scholarship is so persistently thin. Indeed, the Sunday school class may represent "the most wasted hour of the week." However, the staying power is amazing; no more workable approach to Christian training has been introduced and, for better or worse, Sunday school is an operative mark of most local Protestant churches. On its own turf, the Sunday school has enjoyed more success than failure. In fact, religious reformers of all varieties, social revolutionaries, and civil rights champions would do well to familiarize themselves with Sunday school lore. This is true for two reasons.

First, the movement in earlier decades had a decisive role in shaping institutions and attitudes which are today targets for actual or would-be changemakers. For example, the maintenance of racial separation—which equals racism—was by word and deed nurtured by the Sunday school in periods when strides toward racial interaction could have been most beneficial. And the Protestant work ethic with its almost holy views of competition and prosperity (adopted by immigrant groups as intensely American) was succored in nineteenth-century Sunday schools. Moreover, an anti-Roman Catholic bias was imprinted on many minds by the Sunday training. When blacks strike out against the systemic violence of social structures, or when Catholics challenge laws banning public aid to their schools, both are in part pitted against points of view honed in Sunday schools.

Second, despite all the criticism heaped upon it, the Sunday school emerged as a reform movement and so continued for years. It shared with labor and civil rights movements the hallmark of reform ideology: the hope and confident expectation of a better future. The British Sunday school originally sought to reform both the ignorant poor and a society which ignored the educational needs of the poor. In America the reforming was aimed at illiterates, immigrants, Democrats, alcohol drinkers, assorted "sinners," and whoever else did not happen to share the Sunday school's enthusiasms. In the Anglo-American world the Sunday school prospered as part of Protestantism's "benevolent empire"—out to convert the world by starting with the community at hand.

The story is not infrequently self-righteous and paternalistic; more than a few regrettable and reprehensible incidents can be recorded. Still the Sunday school is a rather good object lesson in how a reform movement succeeds, how success transforms the movement, how the progress of one generation becomes the burden of the next, and how reformers have a way of making new, rigid orthodoxies as though the future should not contain the flexibility they themselves required. The course of the movement's particular thrusts is all the more important because Sunday school became an exportable commodity, sent with missionaries around the globe.

As the major popular vehicle for Protestants, the Sunday school has done some remarkable things. It led toward public, universal education. By reversing its own concept of infants as repositories of original sin, it helped in paving the way for childhood as a time of carefree innocence. Today, it continues as the major educational setting where Protestants are confronted with and urged to question the meaning of destiny and death. Approaches may often have been bluntly otherworldly or illusive, but death has been mentioned—something a public school does not, perhaps cannot, do. And the Sunday school has periodically captured and channeled aspirations of the Protestant majority by offering needed definitions of motives and goals.

Schools on Sundays, of course, have appeared in non-Protestant churches. Catholics sometimes started them in frontier days and more than a few synagogues have Sunday classes for youngsters. But by and large the story is Protestant, for Sunday schools never became the rule in American Catholicism or normative in Judaism. Protestants in the nineteenth century built the public school system to suit themselves, since they often considered non-Protestants aliens at best. Then, with tax-supported general education to their liking, Protestants could settle for weekly religious instruction on Sunday mornings. Catholics found such a scheme unacceptable and developed their own parochial system as a substitute for both public and Sunday schools.

Evoking nostalgia and sweet memory as well as criticism, the Sunday school chronicle stands as an illuminating American epic—too long brushed aside. In the progression from the Sunday school's beginnings to the last third of the twentieth century, a virtual overview of what a nation has thought of itself comes to light.

The Big Little School

CHAPTER I

An Idea Whose Time Had Come

*The Sunday school: an institution "eminently
adapted to promote the intellectual and moral
culture of the nation, to perpetuate our republican
and religious institutions, and to reconcile
eminent national prosperity with moral purity
and future blessedness."*
> —From a resolution of the American
> Sunday School Union, 1828

The prospect of reconciling "national prosperity with moral
purity and future blessedness" is a distinctively American
dream, if not obsession. Prosperity and purity—not merely one,
but both in full measure—have formed a constant quest from
Plymouth Colony to the urban wastes of the twentieth century.
Fittingly, Lyman Beecher, a major architect of nineteeth-century evangelical Protestantism, drafted the 1828 resolution in
which the Sunday school took up the dream. Such reconciliation
was, in a sense, the holy grail for Beecher and his luminous
progeny Henry Ward Beecher and Harriet Beecher Stowe. Today,
political and religious rhetoric echoes the prosperity-purity-
blessedness triumphalism of the young nation's spiritual men-

tors. Of course, some modern Americans may wonder whether prosperity and purity can be united. Not Lyman Beecher. For him the coupling was necessary if the United States was to fulfill its true destiny. Future prosperity seemed certain; purity was another matter.

How were "purity" and "future blessedness' to be nurtured? That was *the* question for churchmen of Beecher's stripe in the 1820s, a decade of mingled anxiety and hope. Colonial ways of thinking were outdated and feelings of uneasiness and displacement were developing. State churches, which had earlier symbolized stable morals and manners, were almost completely disestablished, with Connecticut separating the two spheres in 1818 and Massachusetts holding out only until 1833. Beecher was troubled by the loss of an established church as he labored in New England, disturbed that the visible sign of the old order was vanishing before the outline of a new order was yet clear.

Education was poised between old and new. From the past came the conviction, simply stated by Benjamin Rush, the Philadelphia physician who signed the Declaration of Independence: ". . . the only foundation for a useful education in a republic is to be laid in Religion. Without this there can be no virtue, and without virtue there can be no liberty, and liberty is the object and life of all republican government."[1] How could that foundation be laid when, for instance, a Connecticut school visitor in the 1820s found most teachers neglecting prayers? No attempt was made in many schools to offer religious or moral instruction. Catechisms were sometimes recited but scripture was used primarily for reading exercises without note or comment.

Beecher and his fellows, mostly latter-day Puritans, were not inclined to tolerate such casual disregard. Still troubled by the alleged antireligious temper of the French Revolution, they saw a landscape filled with actual and imagined enemies. They were aware of living in a new raw country, bounded on the West by an immense frontier and perched on the edge of an Atlantic basin where fewer allies than challengers put to sea.

Nonetheless, the era was one of fresh breezes, of new possibilities. To use the evangelical explanation, the Spirit was moving along the eastern seacoast and on the frontier. One sign of the

Spirit was the Second Great Awakening whose urgency swept eastward from revival camp meetings in Kentucky and Tennessee during the period from 1795 to 1836. The impact of an 1801 spiritual outbreak at Cane Ridge, Kentucky, was enormous: "It was a spasm among the populace, a violent explosion of emotions which for long had been seeking release, an overwhelming portent for the future of the continent."[2] Apprehension was aroused in some eastern quarters by western revivalism, but the East was also stirred by the evangelical conviction that the Holy Spirit was moving God's people to test new possibilities.

New possibilities included new educational institutions, the Protestant theological seminary and the Sunday school. Innovations of the 1810s, both came to prominence in the 1820s, almost simultaneously becoming permanent parts of the pattern and setting—the ecology—of Protestant education. Seminaries emerged as the national institutions for training leaders; Sunday schools were for local people. After the war of 1812, an apparently spontaneous eruption of Sunday schools occurred along the Atlantic seaboard, especially in New England and New York. Hamlets as well as cities were hit by the idea whose time had come.

The idea of Sunday instruction, however, was not created *de novo* in the early 1800s. How old was it? Who was the founder? These were questions in an active guessing game in the heyday of the Sunday school. Genealogical gamesmanship is often a sign of institutional vitality. In this game the British held the edge. The beginnings went back to Robert Raikes in the 1780s. If not Raikes, then Englishmen could point to Hannah Ball, a pious Methodist who gathered a "wild little company" in her home for Sunday instruction as early as 1763. Naturally, Americans claimed the true "first" for the New World, and they thrust forth Methodist founder John Wesley, as English as could be, but reputed to have instructed children on Sunday as early as 1735 while a missionary in Georgia.

Other reported firsts included a mid-eighteenth-century German pietist community in Ephrata, Pennsylvania, and Washington, Connecticut, where in the early 1780s church elders gathered children on the town green to give training in the Bible and Westminster Catechism. Farther south, "In 1787 George Daughaday, a Methodist preacher in Charleston, South Carolina, was drenched with water pumped from a public cistern 'for the crime of conducting a Sunday-school for the benefit of the African children in that vicinity.' "[3] The games go on. Doubtless, many pastors and laymen carried on some sort of instruction on Sunday in many places during the eighteenth century. United States Sunday instruction in 1820 was something old, something new and plenty borrowed—from Great Britain. The American beginnings cannot be understood apart from what was happening across the Atlantic.

Schools for the Poor

The work of Robert Raikes, known as the "father of the Sunday school," began in the 1780s and quickly spread through the English-speaking world. The Gloucester newspaper publisher became an evangelical celebrity. London and Toronto have statues of him; schools—and a few horses—have borne his name; and one enthusiastic neighbor considered Raikes the most important man since the sixteenth-century Protestant Reformers. All this because he decided to educate poor children on the Lord's Day.

Raikes' Gloucester, on the eve of the Industrial Revolution, was a smallish city. The factory system was preshadowed in at least one large pin-making shop. Like most cities in Georgian England, Gloucester was a pit of misery, flooded by people from the countryside and exposing the children of the growing urban proletariat to constant abuse, both casual and entrenched. Few, if any, schools existed for these youngsters since most of their "betters" believed education of the poor was economically unsound and socially destructive. The only education was in "charity" or "ragged schools," favorite forms of benevolence among a few courageous and wealthy aristocrats. But most children of the poor worked long hours in factories for six days of the week. Sunday was the day when bands of wandering, unsupervised and often lawless children inflicted damage on the outlying areas. Raikes wrote in his Gloucester *Journal* in 1783, "Farmers and other inhabitants of the towns and villages, complain that they receive more injury in their property on the Sabbath than all the week besides."

What could have been more natural than for the observant and benevolent Raikes to start a Sunday charity school? Some cynics have disputed the purity of his motives, ascribing his benevolence to annoyance with noisy children who interrupted his Sunday proofreading of newscopy. But that is a jaundiced view. More likely reasons for his interest in Sunday school were inspiration and logic that have persisted in the movement. Soon after Raikes succeeded his father as publisher of the *Journal* in 1757 he committed himself to jail reform and the moral education of criminals. His attention moved from *crime* to *ignorance* as a cause of crime and then to *children* and their ignorance. Raikes gradually developed a preoccupation with reforming the "morals of the lower class." Or, in modern terms, he wanted to shape preventive measures against juvenile delinquency.

Such logic has appealed to many adults over the past two centuries. For example, J. Edgar Hoover, Director of the Federal Bureau of Investigation, used the same basic argument in his campaign to keep the Sunday school strong. Raikes, of course, was no eighteenth-century crimefighter. He was a gentleman of his day and a person of genial benevolence. He started his first Sunday charity school in 1780 or 1781 by hiring a teacher to set up shop in Gloucester's Sooty Alley. A few years later he wrote of pleasure received in "discovering genius and innate good dispositions among this little multitude." Describing the children, he told a correspondent, "Since the establishment of Sunday schools . . . they are not the ignorant creatures they were before. They are also become more tractable and obedient, and less quarrelsome and revengeful."[4]

No one knows exactly how the transformation in morals which Raikes pointed out was accomplished by Sunday charity schools. It was a complex blend: (1) an unusual adult interest and encouragement, (2) upper-class benevolence with its inevitable measures of condescension, bribery and social coercion, (3) the freedom to learn to read, a remarkable occurrence in the lives of the poor, and (4) a pervasive religious orientation. Raikes was a devout, loyal member of the Church of England. An alumna of

Raikes' school later remembered that the founder was "always at church himself" and listened to the children say the Collect for the day "and whoever said it best had a penny."

Conditions in almost all English cities called for something like the Sunday school. When others heard the reports, they picked up the idea. A movement was in the making. William Fox, a London draper and pious Baptist, was particularly enthusiastic. The Sunday school seemed to be the method for realizing his dream of a systematic, universal, scriptural education for the poor. Unable to draw the interest of the established order, Fox made a personal pledge to the goal of teaching all poor Englishmen to read. He was startled "that in a Christian country, a Protestant country too, no provision would be made for the education of poor children, about whom the heathen take so much pain."[5] In 1785, along with several influential men, Fox formed the first organization promoting Sunday schools, "A Society for the establishment and support of Sunday-schools throughout the kingdom of Great Britain." Its purposes are illuminating: "To prevent vice, to encourage industry and virtue, to dispel the ignorance of darkness, to diffuse the light of knowledge, *to bring men cheerfully to submit to their stations."* [Italics added]

Fox's society raised money to hire teachers, provided Bibles and other needed books and appointed school visitors. It was, in effect, a miniature school system throughout England, although accomplishments of the weekly sessions were less grand than the onslaught against the "ignorance of darkness" mentioned by Fox. The London Society taught reading but not writing. Manual laborers needed to read, according to one of Fox's fellow philanthropists, in order to learn religion and fill up vacant hours but writing was not "necessary or expedient." The benefactors apparently feared that if the poor learned to write, the new-found talent might be used to foment civil strife. Sunday school sponsors agreed that the poor must be kept in their place. Fox himself explained, "There is no intention of raising them [the children] above their common level; for in that case how would our manufactories be carried on, our houses erected and our tables furnished?" The Archbishop of Canterbury, speaking with a society member in 1786, was reported to have noted that "Sunday schools were well adapted to improve the morals of the common people."

Nor were the poor allowed to forget the benevolence of sponsors. Jonas Hanway's 1786 Sunday school manual, first of a long line of such publications, said that "scholars" must be told that a "number of the clergy, nobility, gentry, and others have taken you under their protection. They wish to make you wise." Teachers were supposed to tell pupils, "I am accountable to God and to your benefactors, to do you justice, and to see that none of you be idle and worthless."[6] Soberly conservative, the early Sunday school benefactors retained stiff class lines along with feelings of generosity toward individuals. Their sensitivity to the plight of the poor was unusual for their rank, yet more intense was a desire *not* to be misunderstood by pupils, potential backers or enemies.

The growth of the Sunday charity schools was phenomenal in the 1780s. Enrollment was about 250,000 children by 1787. Raikes' influence as journalist and publicist was helpful in expanding the concept, as was Fox's Society. But the more important cause of the enormous popularity and growth came from the people themselves and the consent of society. For the poor, schools on Sunday represented a start toward a better life. One commoner, asked if he could read, replied, "No sir, I was born in the days in which there were no Sunday schools; but my children can read very prettily."[7] Unlike the older charity institutions, Sunday schools did not incur the hostility or resentment of the poor and they served as an antidote to the church's apathy about religious education. Above all, the Sunday school was an inexpensive way of meeting the educational needs of the common people in England's growing industrial society. Labor was disciplined during the week and religion controlled on Sunday. Nobody's ox was gored, or so it seemed then.

The "Benevolent Empire"

Carrying the Sunday school forward was an evangelical thrust toward a Protestant "benevolent empire." Led by William Wilberforce, the Clapham group set the pace in the Church of England. The Anglican evangelicals were as responsible as the

Wesleys and their Methodist societies for the "unmistakable improvement in manners and morals of early nineteeth-century England." Wilberforce's "earnest but slight efforts" around 1790 expanded in twenty-five years into "an immense reform movement, well organized and superbly directed . . . and using agencies and resources of a size, number and power not yet fully recognized."[8]

Only slight overstatement is found in the following description of the British "benevolent empire" of which the Sunday school became one part:

> There were societies for putting down gin-mills and Sunday fairs and closing cook-shops on Sundays, for sending Bibles, homilies and Prayer Books everywhere and for keeping country girls at home. There were societies for educating infants, and adults, and juveniles, and orphans, and female orphans, and adult orphans, and nearly everybody else, according to the formularies of the Established Church or not according to them but always according to some religious formularies. There were societies for the deaf and dumb, for the insane, for the blind, for the ruptured, for the scrofulous, for the club-footed, for the penitent syphilitic and for the impenitent syphilitic; for legitimate children and illegitimate children, for chimney sweepers' apprentices and against Tom Paine and Shelley; in aid of juvenile prostitutes and against juvenile mendicants; for distressed respectable widows, for poor pious clergymen in the country, for poor females in the maritime districts, for distressed foreigners, for small debtors, for prisoners, for female émigrées, for the deserving poor, for respectable married women and disreputable unmarried women, for sick people in hospitals and sick people out of hospitals, and for simple ordinary sick strangers. . . . Above all there were societies to suppress.[9]

The Sunday school was just one small expression of this incredible voluntary effort. In 1803, for example, two societies were founded: The Society for Superseding the Necessity of Climbing Boys, and the Sunday School Union of London—the latter soon to eclipse Fox's society as the nerve center for a burgeoning enterprise. Although many of its strongest schools were sponsored by Dissenters (Methodists and others), the movement's destiny, at least for a time, was largely in the hands of Anglican evangelicals.

Women were notable in this company. That was nothing new in Sunday school circles, for Sarah Trimmer, a contemporary of Raikes and writer of "exemplary tales" for children, was an early champion of the cause. She was a visitor with the royal family and extolled the virtues of the new undertaking to Queen Charlotte, wife of George III. The greatest woman evangelical was Hannah More, a lieutenant in the Wilberforce group and a literary light of the eighteenth century admired by Samuel Johnson. Along with her sister she organized a string of schools in Somerset in which more than 20,000 children of the lower classes learned the habits of industry and piety.

As the Sunday school was taken under the wing of the Wilberforcian coalition, it was attacked by the nonevangelical party within the Established Church. The Archbishop of Canterbury's benign approval of the 1780s lapsed. Sunday classes were accused of being "nurseries of fanaticism," which plainly translated meant the establishment feared sentiments favorable to the French Revolution, that "virus" of the 1790s which Englishmen wanted confined beyond the Channel. The Bishop of Rochester despaired. "Schools of *atheism* and *disloyalty,*" he said, *"abound* in this country; schools in the shape and disguise of charity schools and SUNDAY SCHOOLS, in which the minds of the children of the very lowest orders are enlightened; that is to say, taught to despise religion, and the laws, and all subordination."[10]

The bishop's heady and undeserved charge was exactly the kind Raikes, Fox and their collaborators feared, the reason they had disavowed any intent to alter the class system. The unsavory reputation which the Sunday schools acquired for a time had less to do with the French Revolution, however, than with English ecclesiastical politics. High churchmen were in part sniping at the Methodists and indirectly assaulting the evangelicals within the Established Church who had taken up the Sunday school cause. An attack on Wilberforce was the real purpose. Controversy so thickened that as the nineteeth century replaced the eighteenth, Prime Minister William Pitt had to be dissuaded from asking Parliament to suppress the Sunday school.

Opposition did not faze the English evangelicals. They were

sustained by a vision providing energy and a sense of rightness about their cause. Their intent, as historian Robert Kelly has said, was to "bring personal purity and sincerity back into private and public life" not by philosophical arguments about moral laws "but by creating in their hearers a cataclysmic sense of their own personal depravity. Only when men were aghast at their own individual barbarism, and convinced thereby of their inevitable destiny in hell, could they begin properly to realize what Evangelicals described as the sweet gifts opened out to them by the forgiving love and sacrifice of Jesus Christ."[11]

An Anglo-American Community

The pattern in which Sunday schools were taken over by empire-building evangelicals was repeated in America. Benevolent individuals in the New World, however, borrowed the model of Sunday charity schools from Britain before the Wilberforce group took over the leadership. Just seven years after the end of the Revolutionary War—about a decade after Raikes' first school opened—prominent Philadelphians formed the First Day Society. The Pennsylvania organization was almost a carbon copy of the society launched by Fox, though the borrowing had to be done discreetly in the period of anglophobia following the war. Echoing the intentions of Raikes and Fox, the First Day Society set about to instruct "the offsprings of indigent parents" on Sunday, a day which is often "employed to the worst of purposes, the depravity of morals and manners."

Philadelphia's Sunday school society marked the start of a common school system for the children of that city's poor and its work was an early experiment in American pluralism. Sponsors included Dr. Rush, a Universalist layman as well as physician and Founding Father, Mathew Carey, Roman Catholic layman, and William White, the Protestant Episcopal Bishop of Pennsylvania. Bishop White heard of Sunday schools when he went to London for his consecration and was one of those transporting the idea to America. Imitation of British Sunday school ways continued in the new nation through the 1790s and into the early decades of the nineteenth century. At the same time, the move-

ment increasingly came under the evangelical umbrella which
meant that pluralistic coalitions of sponsors were not to prevail
in the unfolding history. An Anglo-American community of
shared attitudes was developing during that same period between evangelicals facing one another across the North Atlantic.
Despite the enormous distance, uncertain mails and fractures
created by the parting of 1776, members of this community
"visited one another, . . . founded great circles of transatlantic
families, and launched into reform movements in church and
secular society together."[12] Frequently, the evangelical network
coincided with commercial and economic patterns. Philadelphia, New York and Boston were the American cities where Sunday schools first flourished. In these seaports many emerging
Sunday school leaders were merchants in touch with the British.

The extent and importance of intercontinental evangelical ties
for the American "benevolent empire" in general and the Sunday school in particular are illustrated by the experience of two
ladies of the same New York family. The multiple concerns of
Isabella Graham and her daughter Joanne Bethune demonstrated creative borrowing from Britain and the beginnings of a
bewildering array of benevolent agencies, generally nondenominational and pulsating with evangelical fervor. The Graham-
Bethune career also shows the continuation in America of the
precedent of women's leadership set by Sarah Trimmer and Hannah More in England.

Mrs. Graham kept in close touch with her friends in Scotland.
"The interchange of pious sentiments," as her biographer gently
put it, was valued on both sides of the Atlantic. When she received sermons, tracts and reports on revivals from abroad, Mrs.
Graham gathered her friends to share the news and to pray for
guidance about their responsibilities in America. These inter-
changes produced such efforts as a society for sending missionaries to Indians and poor settlers on the frontier and the "Society
for the Relief of Poor Widows with Small Children," forerunner
of the New York Orphan Asylum.

Sunday schools in America got an extra boost after Mrs. Bethune visited Scotland early in the nineteenth century. She discovered the Edinburgh Gratis Sabbath-School Society, and so

found a new cause for America. Following much correspondence with friends in England, she brought about the Female Union for the Promotion of Sabbath Schools in New York City in 1816. The constitution was lifted from the Bristol Sunday School Union with "very few alterations." Plagiarism of purpose and structure was frequent.

The women Sunday school advocates of the early years were not avowedly, or perhaps even self-consciously, plugging for their own empowerment or recognition. But they were taking advantage of one of the few places in church life where women's initiative was possible. Mrs. Bethune put the word "female" in the title of her organization deliberately. She was, however, hesitant in unfurling her female union since some unanswered questions lurked around the Sunday school. Should one engage in a covert form of Sabbath-breaking by teaching? Much of the New York clergy was indifferent to the question as well as to the Sunday school movement while laymen were slow to respond to Mrs. Bethune's appeals for support. Mr. Bethune is said to have finally told his wife there was no "use in waiting for the men" and that she should gather ladies of "different denominations"[13] to begin the work themselves. Fairness requires the addition that her husband was instrumental in starting the New York Sunday School Union Society, limited to male benefactors.

The backing of "pious women" was generally helpful when the Sunday school met opposition, as it did occasionally from clergy and laymen. A typical example of resistance occurred in 1817 in Medway, Massachusetts, where women wanted a school. The young minister withheld his nod almost as long as the deacons. Skeptical men commented, "These young folks are taking too much upon themselves"; and with a shrug of sarcasm some said, "These women will be in the pulpit next."[14]

In the Sunday classrooms the women were, indeed, increasingly found, telling the "exemplary tales" of Sarah Trimmer and other British writers whose materials they cheerfully plundered. American evangelicals needed tracts and books for the children of seaport or frontier towns and they produced little independent literature until later in the nineteenth century. It is rather amusing to imagine a boy in western Pennsylvania in 1817 reading such indubitably English fare as "Tom Trifles and Peter Player," a grim story about sloth, but such material was provided. For all the humor and the accompanying embarrassment, the dissimilarities of a frontier lad in America and a London youngster are less important for the history of the Sunday school than the experience and sense of common purpose shared by the transatlantic evangelicals.

A Margin of Difference

Differences in British and American Sunday schools began to emerge in the 1820s. Despite the similarities in evangelical point of view and the American borrowing, departures were inevitable in the New World. The first margin of difference was in constituencies. The early nineteenth-century English Sunday schools remained, for all practical purposes, institutions for children of the poor. Those in America became more inclusive.

In 1889 the Lord Mayor of London recalled that when he was growing up around mid-century many of the lower class received their education in Sunday schools. The one-day charity institution long continued as the creation of benevolence in which all concerned were constantly aware of the social distance between donor and recipient. An 1813 public notice inviting poor parents to send their children to Sunday school and berating them for not doing so earlier began, "It is much to be lamented, that while the Benevolent and Humane are exerting themselves for your Children's Benefit, that you should be so careless of their best Interests." Forty years later the sentiment had not yet disappeared.

The initial American Sunday schools, such as those of the Philadelphia First Day Society, were devoted almost exclusively to instructing the poor in reading and writing. A class-oriented enterprise could not survive long, however, in a nation priding itself on democratic equality. Class differences, of course, existed in the national period following the War of 1812, but explicit focus on class lines among whites was unpopular. (All twenty-two states in 1820 had *caste* rather than *class* systems when it came to black-white relations. The main difference between the eleven free and eleven slave states was in the legal definition of caste.) The poor were uninterested in special schools for themselves. "The feeling that it was intended for *the poor*, kept both the poor and the rich from attending it," a churchman said of a Pittsburgh Sunday school in 1809.[15]

Pragmatic founding fathers of the American Sunday school tried the opposite tack. When Lyman Beecher was an old man looking back, he explained how he and others prevented the Sunday school's ruination when they realized the poor would not go. He went to the best families in town, imploring them to send their children to the Sunday schools to mingle with the poor. The persuasive clergyman won some supporters, dispatched his own brood and the plan worked, giving "an unheard of impetus"[16] to the Sunday school and reforming its role.

Similar rescue operations apparently happened with considerable frequency wherever there were Sunday schools. What had begun as an exercise in charity was converted into a prep school for the whole of evangelical America. Was the reform Beecher described simply a ploy to get the children of the poor into a school on Sunday? That conclusion cannot be totally rejected but something more significant, more rooted in the social fabric, was taking place. The myths and realities of American democracy were concentrating in the Sunday school, which was to become a wellspring for the culture considered most American in the eyes of the rest of the world. In a keen observation, one analyst has said that the Sunday school was being upgraded to the "level of middle class respectability which some Americans had attained and the rest refused to admit that they could not attain. On Saturday night the poor scrubbed up. The next morning they dressed up and presented themselves at Sunday school to prove they were just as good as anybody else. It is a tribute to American society that they were received at face value—but that face had to be clean."[17]

At the same time that men like Lyman Beecher were trying to save the Sunday schools by mixing the clientele, the slow spread of public schools was having the same effect. When public schools opened—and it was a slow process—the Sunday schools were freed of the taint of "charity" and released from pressure to teach reading and writing. Religious instruction alone became the main undertaking.

Not incidentally, the shift in focus and function had important consequences for relations of white and black children in northern Sunday schools. As long as the schools were largely for the children of the poor, mixing the races was no great difficulty. The introduction of an inclusiveness cutting across white class lines made the presence of black children embarrassing and troublesome. Only a few integrated schools existed in the North. Generally speaking, the American Sunday school movement faithfully observed the culture's caste demarcations just as the English evangelicals reflected the class lines there. A recorder at the London Sunday School Union penned the following account of a report made by a visiting American on work in Philadelphia:

Among other schools there was . . . one for the little chimney sweeps who were all in that country children of colour—he did not mean from the nature of their occupation (a laugh) but that they were naturally born so, and the effect of the Sunday schools on this previously-neglected class of children was really astonishing—they had formerly been among the most debased and ignorant classes of persons in the whole city of Philadelphia; but now such an alternation has taken place that the Song of Solomon might be heard from their lips as they passed along to their morning work.[18]

While a widespread and probably unconscious acceptance of caste barriers prevailed in the North, the South was slow to adopt the Sunday school, partly because it was identified, indeed often equated, with black education. After 1831 southern whites had the memory of Nat Turner's revolt to remind them of what literacy and uncontrolled black religion could stir up. The image of Sunday schools as places to educate blacks is probably one reason Baptists in the South were reluctant to enter the movement, and Sunday school work in Mississippi proceeded very slowly.

In sum, the margin of difference between the English and American Sunday schools which could be seen in the 1820s grew wider as the reality and challenge of the West came crashing in upon the New World Protestant consciousness during the third and fourth decades of the nineteenth century. The frontier—the vast reaches of the Mississippi Valley—held the future nexus of power which would finally determine the young nation's destiny.

Men such as Lyman Beecher knew the scepter was passing from East to West. If the religious and republican institutions were not perpetuated beyond the Appalachian Mountains then reconciliation of prosperity and purity would not be continued. Beecher was not unmindful of the coming crisis as he penned those words in 1828 lauding the Sunday school as reconciler of prosperity and purity and sending it forth as promoter of the "intellectual and moral culture of the nation."

CHAPTER II

In Every Destitute Place

An excitement has gone forth.
    —A frontiersman, speaking of the Sunday school

To win and hold the United States for evangelical Protestantism, the "benevolent empire" had to move westward. The Sunday school was a major vehicle for the trek. Log cabin pioneers, first on the frontier, had nature's garden, powder and shot, weather and Indian worries—and the Sunday school. Transient as the rough life itself, it often followed the stouthearted who broke for high timber. Field-to-field settlers who came after the pioneers found in the schools a sense of contact with "back home," scarce books and the promise of culture. When businessmen, the third wave of frontiersmen, arrived, they found Sunday schools as established landmarks.

The Sunday school was there so early and fared so well west of the Applachians that most editors of American history texts and popularizers of frontier manners treat it as normal early American scenery. Yet the process of its spread was neither automatic nor easy. The American Sunday School Union, launched in Philadelphia in 1824, was the "benevolent empire" agency vowing to make sure instruction in morals and faith was available when dry goods merchants brought their bolts to hamlets north of Cincinnati.

In 1830 the American Sunday School Union took on a staggering task, one which, though never fully carried out, furnished the challenge needed to forge a movement. Within two years, and "in reliance upon divine aid," the organization resolved to establish "a Sunday school in every destitute place where it is practicable, throughout the Valley of the Mississippi."[1] The call to the "Valley campaign" and the warm approval by the General Assembly of the Presbyterian Church meeting at the same time were acts of bravado. The Mississippi Valley, as they defined it, stretched from Harrisburg, Pennsylvania, to the Rocky Mountains, from Canada to the Gulf of Mexico. It covered more than two-thirds of what was then the land mass of the nation.

This grandiose *two-year* plan was laid by a new, largely volunteer organization with a three-man staff. Some well-to-do laymen backed the thrust but it was still a shoestring operation progressing mainly on the enthusiasm of its volunteers. The campaign itself provided heroes necessary for the movement. Sunday school conventions from 1830 on thrilled to hear reports of missionaries who had valiantly encountered physical hardships, infidels, "Romanists" and scoffers. The romance of the western experience sustained the morale of volunteers working in more humdrum circumstances. For here was a new cause, a common task embraced by both those who ventured West and the others who stayed home.

The Valley campaign was only one effort to win the West for true patriotism and religion. Five nondenominational societies, each with a part in the shaping of the West, were developed between 1815 and 1826 with a strong core of Congregationalists and Presbyterians in alliance with occasional Methodists, Episcopalians and Baptists. The American Sunday School Union was one. Another, founded in Boston in 1815 to subsidize the training of future ministers, was the American Education Society, which shaped the traditional pattern of theological education; still another, the American Home Missionary Society, was set up in New York in 1826 to assist poor congregations in paying pastors and to send ministers to new western settlements. In 1816 the American Bible Society was established in New York to distribute the Testaments, millions of which went to the frontier before 1861; and in the same city nine years later appeared the American Tract Society which issued some 200 million books and tracts prior to the Civil War.

All five societies enjoyed certain common characteristics including a "union principle," earnest founders who sensed impending crisis and the potency of the immediate future, and a determination to discover and hone new strategies. The Valley campaign of the Sunday School Union reflected these marks of the nineteenth-century reform spirit.

"A More Perfect Union"

Evangelical penetration of the Mississippi Valley would have been impossible apart from the "union principle." Leaders of the five societies knew the frontier was too big for any one agency or denomination to win alone; therefore, a cooperative strategy was warp and woof of relations among the organizations themselves. They naturally competed for support while their activities were necessarily complementary. The field was a place of constantly interlacing responsibilities. A Sunday school worker, sent by the Union, distributed Bibles and tracts furnished by other groups. Any Sunday school could become the nucleus for a possible congregation to be organized by the Home Missionary Society which by 1831 had 463 western missionaries promoting the full range of the societies' interests. When Missionary Society personnel started Sunday schools they reported directly to the Union in Philadelphia.

The "union principle" was generally a glittering idea during early nineteenth-century decades when the United States— *the* Union—was in the making. No one doubted the reality of religious and political differences, yet unity amid diversity was the paramount hope of the Sunday School Union and others. From within this perspective, the Sunday school strategy was straightforward and unabashedly stated: To ignore, whenever possible, doctrinal and political differences; to be antiseptically *un-denominational* in purpose and practice.

The un-denominational nature was to be questioned later. It seemed essential in the 1830s. Establishment of Sunday schools "in every destitute place" in the sparsely settled Valley was utterly inconceivable, even suicidal, if approached denominationally. Even when the "moral power and religious influence" of all favorably disposed residents were concentrated in a union school," said a Union report, that combined power was "but feebly felt upon the heterogeneous character, and unsettled habits of the surrounding population." The evangelicals were advised to leave their "distinctive pecularities out of sight, and out of mind"[2] for the sake of teaching the cardinal truths of Christianity. In the pre-ecumenical nineteenth century, necessity and prudence—"out of sight" and "out of mind"—were the most advanced ecumenical ways of working. Caution, and perhaps expediency, was quite clear in instruction given to Sunday school missionaries and in the way libraries were promoted.

The agents assigned to the West in 1832 were charged to be "particularly careful to avoid all controversy or disputes with any who differ from yourself in religious opinions. By all means avoid every thing like sectarism, or remarks that would in their tendency, wound the feelings of any Christian. . . . *On the delicate question of slavery, abstain from all remarks; much injury may result from an indiscreet observation."* The overriding goal was "to bring every child and youth . . . under the influence of the gospel."[3] Consequently, a tactic of silence and inoffensiveness on social and political questions was judged imperative. Slavery was taboo because it was the most bitter public issue and the most likely to rend a society or school. The Sunday school movement and evangelical Protestantism in general would long be delicate about slavery; delicate, too, after slavery was replaced by organized discrimination. For the most part, Sunday schools were late in discovering a gospel reason for racial equality.

The nonpartisan temper was maintained in the Union's program for gathering and promoting Sunday school libraries. A committee of laymen representing the major denominations made the selections, and any one member could block a publication that violated his denominational sensibilities. This sort of veto politics was necessary if the Sunday School Union was to maintain diplomatic relations with the warring tribes of American Protestants. Juvenile books, for example, were "fitted to children and youth of all classes and characters; they have nothing in them offensive to denominational, sectional, or political preferences, or prejudices."[4]

This strenuous effort to be inoffensive was both praised and criticized. Robert Baird, the great nineteenth-century American church historian, approved the Sunday School Union publications since, lacking anything "repugnant" to doctrines of any evangelical denomination, they were a boon to Christian education in places where churches were too small to act alone. Despite its anxious caution, however, the Union aroused the apprehensions of other churchmen and sometimes met reprisals. Notably unimpressed were those who believed the Valley campaign was part of a covert Presbyterian plot to capture the allegiance of the younger generation. Various non-Presbyterians got the impression that crucial leadership of the Union always turned out to be Presbyterian. Some such suspicion must have crossed the minds of those forming the Methodist Sunday-School Union in 1827. The General Protestant Episcopal Sunday School Union, established in 1826, was another countermove against the ambitious reach of the "un-denominational" agency. Episcopal Bishop William Meade praised the "noble" Sunday School Union but regretted that its material failed to put forth the distinctive traits of the "different denominations connected with the Gospel."[5]

No matter how inoffensive the "union principle" was made, the denomination-oriented churchmen would not be deflected from the chance to shape educational institutions, influence loyalties of the young, increase profits of big business religious publishing, and gain new congregations in the West. But in the 1830s and 1840s American-style denominations were relatively new inventions of Protestant life just coming into their own. Denominational Sunday school unions, which later evolved into boards of Christian education, had not yet gained power in the 1830s. The initiative then rested with the small group directing the American Sunday School Union. Its compelling vision of the future demanded that the West be won lest it be conquered by barbarism. Reverberations of the crusade were long felt in mainstream American culture, Protestant and non-Protestant, where the Sunday school deposited its particular version of the dream of prosperity and purity.

The Threat of Barbarism

The Valley campaign stirred up considerable attention along the Atlantic seaboard in 1830 and 1831. Mass meetings, such as one in Philadelphia which raised over $5,000, were not uncommon. The most interesting gathering spurred by the Sunday school resolution was a joint session of the United States Congress on February 16, 1831. President Andrew Jackson, who was sick, sent regrets, but a host of congressmen and senators assembled to discuss Sunday schools and the West. On the motion of Francis Scott Key, author of the future national anthem, Senator Felix Grundy of Tennessee presided. The senator was a vice president of the Sunday School Union, but his wife holds an even greater distinction in the early history of the movement. In 1820 Mrs. Grundy founded the first Sunday school in Nashville, today the undisputed Sunday school capital of the world, with five or six firms turning out enough religious study material to compete with country music as a leading industry.

Members of Congress heard the "every destitute place" resolution and most subsequent comments were favorable, though a few grumbled. Ohio Congressman Elisha Whittlesey hoped the Union resolution did not imply that the people in the Valley were "more subject to depravity, or more debased in morals" than fellow citizens in the East. His touchiness was appropriate in light of the low opinion of westerners reflected in numerous bald and condescending arguments for the campaign advanced in the East. In the famous *Plea for the West,* written in 1835, Lyman Beecher was slightly more sophisticated than some promoters. He contended that the question of whether republican institutions could be reconciled with universal suffrage would be answered in the West and westerners needed help in meeting the challenge, particularly in achieving education of the heart and mind and in perpetuating law and virtue. Beecher was specific about his fears. He said the "danger from uneducated minds is augmenting daily by the rapid influx of foreign emigrants, the greater part unacquainted with our institutions, unaccustomed to self-government, inaccessible to education, and easily accessible to prepossession, and inveterate credulity, and intrigue, and easily embodied and wielded by sinister design."

"Inveterate credulity," "intrigue," and "sinister design"—why these words of darkness and malevolence? Sunday school organizers were willing to speak in such a scarifying vein partly because such talk raised money in the East. But the phrases also disclosed a genuine foreboding over the "barbarism," a double-edged threat to those Sunday school men who were terrified of Catholics and sometimes scandalized by Democrats.

Managers of the national benevolent societies feared that Catholics might come to dominate the Mississippi Valley and might eventually "either control the entire country through the polls or form an alliance with the ungodly and thus make good government impossible."[6] In its 1835 annual report the Sunday School Union complained bitterly about the flood of Catholics moving West. "Catholic Europe is disgorging her priests, nuns, and treasures" in a systematic effort to "control education," said the evangelicals. While such claims were remarkably astute appeals to eastern misconceptions, later "know-nothing" sentiments, and the Anglo-Saxon "Native American" movement, the actual situation was quite different. A flood of Catholic immigrants did arrive after 1830, but most—especially the Irish Americans—stayed in eastern cities. Catholic missionary societies were active on the frontier and Jesuits ever-present; yet Catholic and Protestant numerical strength were nowhere comparable. Protestants had the situation well in hand. For example, the Catholic diocese of Cincinnati, one of the strongest in the West, did not get a sustaining parochial school until 1830 and major educational strides did not come until a quarter-century later.

The inflammatory language and bitter feelings which prevailed between Protestant and Catholic in most places were, ironically, overcome on occasion in joint Sunday school work. In

the 1840s a clergyman, writing to the American Home Missionary Society, reported that German immigrants and Roman Catholics had started a common Sunday school in Dubuque, Iowa.
Doubtless the exacting frontier life prompted many such temporary alliances although, prudently, few were reported to the Sunday School Union in Philadelphia.

Sunday school hierarchs were more discreet in alluding to the
second expression of barbarism. Their reports from the West in
the 1830s were filled with vague references to disorder, uncon-
strained passions and violence. Theodore Frelinghuysen, a New
Jersey politician, warned the Union that the West would soon
lapse into a "universal degeneracy of manners" unless a "refor-
mation of public sentiment" was aided by responsible religious
forces. He was speaking in a code language of a nineteenth-
century churchman worried about subversion. (A code phrase
today is "law and order" and most people know the targets can
be those who dissent as well as those who commit crime.) What
did a serious-minded Protestant in the 1830s mean by "universal
degeneracy of manners?"[7] No explanation can ignore the Whig
clash with the Democrats.

That Andrew Jackson's rise in the West and the expansion of
the "benevolent empire" agencies coincided was no accident.
The election of the general from Tennessee and his raucous
Presidential reception on the night of inauguration made "good
men" and aristocrats worry. A quick response was to press the
evangelical cause in the West; the Sunday School Union's Valley
campaign came little more than a year after President Jackson's
first days in Washington.

Most of the Sunday school leaders were of either Whig or conservative persuasion. Characteristic of the type was Frelinghuysen, presiding officer and chief spokesman for the first national
convention of Sunday school workers in 1832 and a long-time
vice president of the Union. He was an eminent Whig, a U. S.
senator (1829–1835) and, as Whig Vice Presidential candidate in
1844, undertook "to join his Christian talents with the political
ability of Henry Clay in the hope of gaining a victory for conserv-
atism."[8] Most of all, Frelinghuysen was a confirmed opponent of
Jackson, warning "good citizens" against the Democrats and the

danger of being too proud of country and liberties. The senator told the 1835 Sunday School Union meeting that pride and an independent spirit were threatening the rule of law. "Resistance," "liberty," "independence," "rights of man" were, in his estimation, "mere watchwords for licentiousness and all misrule" when they grew too familiar and were applied without sound principles.

Frelinghuysen had a remedy for such ills. The Sunday school, if allowed to do its slow but substantial work, would, he believed, help create a godly people, industrious, reliable and impervious to enticements of mischievous politicians like Jackson. The benevolent managers' anxiety over Democrats, their dread of disorder and chaos, put them in the same camp as the early Sunday school organizers in England. Theodore Frelinghuysen had more in common with Hannah More than an American Whig would have wanted to admit in 1835.

A fretful concern undergirded the American Sunday School Union's efforts in the West well into the 1840s. Reports about the "growing but unformed, chaotic, tumultuating society" were used to bring new pressure on supporters. If only the frontier youths were properly trained, the promoters said, then perhaps the nation's future might be more secure. In short, older America was taking no chances with young America.

Political anxieties alone, however, could never have sustained the Valley campaign for long. Another motivation, beyond the desire to spread eastern morals and Whig politics, was equally compelling. Less spectacular and probably more lasting in its imprint on the Sunday school was the evangelical belief that the deeper meaning of the West and its challenges lay in God's providence. The move to establish Sunday schools in every community was the first step toward a *new missionary future.* Many of the leaders in the 1820s and 1830s saw the American West and the world as simultaneous mission fields in one vast undertaking. The West was decisive. If the Valley could be won, America would be free to fulfill its destiny as the new "new Israel," God's beachhead in his *final* triumphal invasion of the world. The task was clear: Christianize America so America can christianize the world. As an integral part of the evangelical apparatus for soul saving and nation shaping, the Sunday school movement was no mere gesture that could be abandoned when life turned sour and idealism waned. The struggling institution was, at least to its foremost proponents, an instrument of God's choosing, one means of realizing his plan for the world. The Valley campaign was really the thrust of destiny.

The lure of destiny was shared by many along the frontier, even in some of those places easterners judged "destitute." A young St. Louis fur trader wrote to his mother in Connecticut not long after the 1830 Union resolution. After saying he had no regrets in going West he went on:

We are fast growing to a giants statue [sic]. The days of our childhood will soon be past. If nothing but the love of country actuate us something must be done to dispel ignorance & drive away vice. So thought the members of the [Presbyterian] General Assembly when they lately met in Philadelphia. They were however inspired by higher motives. The glory of God & the love of souls influences them. When they passed a resolution to establish Sunday Schools in every settlement in this valley, within the short space of two years, a resolution fraught with greater consequences to the Nation than any ever before adopted.

But why am I speaking of these things. *An excitement has gone forth. An excitement that the power of man can neither gainsay or put down. It exists not in the East alone. It has passed the boundry which separates the East from the Western States. It has reached this place.*

. . . Can teachers but be found to take charge of these schools as they are formed, we may soon hope a different state of things. Sabbath Schools are the only means which the great majority of the people of this State have for the education of their children, and unless these schools are established, books given them, and addequite [sic] teachers found to take charge of them, we cannot expect the children will be any better than their Fathers were. Think it then, My Dear Mother no hardship that you are separated thus far from one of your children but rather rejoice that he is permitted to come & be in some humble part in this great work.[9]

The trapper had many Valley colleagues equally excited by the "great work" and its indisputable role in shaping the future of America and the world. They dreamed of a world where needs are encompassed by benevolence and pledged themselves to make it so. More than anything else, the harnessing of destiny to that dream made the Sunday school forces into a movement.

"A Horse Tempts One to Go too Fast"

"It is an age of great associations, rather than great men," said Gardiner Spring, a New York Presbyterian minister, in explaining the secret of early nineteenth-century evangelical success. He was essentially correct, for the associations and benevolent societies were ingenious and innovative, comparable in the scope of their imaginations to a few civil rights groups of the 1960s. The Sunday School Union, for instance, had a remarkable ability to stretch limited funds over a host of ambitious commitments.

But men and women, not board meetings, did the field work. Some Sunday school workers, particularly women, confined their activities to western home communities but many hundreds became itinerant missionaries ranging over the immense frontier. They were a diverse lot. Sunday school agents were often laymen, though some were ordained; a few had degrees while others claimed two or three years of uncertain schooling; college and seminary students labored during vacations; full-time agents were paid—if at all—the fine sum of one dollar a day; they were hardy and resourceful, if they survived. The life was lonely, transient and exhausting.

The missionaries were urged by the Sunday School Union to walk from village to village. Instructions from Philadelphia said "a horse tempts one to go too fast. Besides the missionary is generally welcome, because he can talk as well as eat. His horse is unwelcome, because he eats but cannot talk." Better than beast or buggy were a walking staff and "a good satchel well stored with specimens of library books, and catalogues to show, and miscellaneous books to sell, and tracts and papers to give away."[10] The Union felt that if the work was done thoroughly, an agent needed to go no faster than an invigorating walk would propel him.

Sunday school nomads needed a quickness in using chance encounters and a blunt, direct approach that might startle later generations of liberal Protestants accustomed to a piety of genteel nondirectiveness. John McCullagh, a scrappy Scottish immigrant, was typical of the masters of the trade. He was known as the "Sunday school man of the South" because of his work in the Kentucky hills. One tale about McCullagh tells of his organizing a school on Buckhorn Creek and then meeting a ragged lad, Archie, who attended no school and whose baby brother had recently died. The account continued with McCullagh asking:

"Would you like to have a book that tells about a happy world up yonder, where people will never die any more?"

"That I would, sir."

"Well, here it is," said the missionary, pulling out a little Testament. "Sit down, Archie, and let me tell you about it."

They sat down on the log, and the mountain-boy drank in every word Mr. McCullagh told him of Christ, heaven and eternal life. The little fellow's heart was touched, and looking up, he said, "What is your name, Mr. Stranger?"

On being told, he said, "I have heard tell of you before. You is the man what makes Sunday-schools, ain't you? I wish I knowed how to read this little book what tells about Jesus."

"Well, my little man, if you will attend the Sunday-school near the bridge, on Buckhorn Creek, they will teach you."[11]

The more colorful missionaries became celebrities in the East where they told of their work and raised money. They regaled audiences with stories about unfordable brooks, wild animals, drunkards, antimissionary Protestants and debates with infidels and freethinkers. The venerable McCullagh was a favorite in the East and, it should be noted, he had a horse.

The most famous frontier agent was Stephen Paxson, who was, according to a Union official, a "plain, unlettered, irreligious mechanic" before he encountered Sunday school. Paxson was dragooned by his daughter into attending a Sunday morning class in a southern Illinois prairie settlement. He stayed with it, was "converted," picked up the rudiments of literacy, became a neighborhood Sunday school organizer, and was spotted as a man of considerable potential by John Adams. "Father Adams"—very much a Protestant—was headmaster of Andover Academy in Massachusetts, and at the age of seventy started a second career as a Sunday school agent in Illinois. Adams encouraged Paxson to apply for a missionary commission in the 1840s.

In the mid-nineteenth century Paxson and his trusty horse, "Raikes," were known in hundreds of hamlets across Illinois and adjoining states. He was, in effect, a "traveling bishop" for the remote sections of the frontier. The missionary took news from one isolated settlement to another, sold his books and materials, distributed tracts and Bibles, taught, counseled, preached, gave Fourth of July orations and organized Sunday schools. In twenty-odd years he established over 1,200 schools, many of which survived and evolved into congregations. Paxson outlined the stages in the process from Sunday school to congregation: "a few papers, books and personal efforts gather in the children; . . . the parents follow; then the prayer-meeting; then the preacher."[12]

Paxson omitted only one step, one not aiming at a congregation but important for communities. That was the arrival of the "schoolmarm" and the common school. Sunday schools were often seedbeds for both church and public education, sometimes being deliberately designed as forerunners of more adequate public school systems. The Indiana Sabbath School Union enunciated precisely such a plan in 1827. "Let Sabbath Schools be established wherever it is practicable," said the policy. "They will answer the double purpose of paving the way for common schools, and of serving as a substitute till they are generally formed. Parents and children, becoming sensible to the sweets and the benefits of learning, will unite in one loud and determined call for the permanent means of education."[13]

Occasionally, and not surprisingly, Sunday schools were pressed into service as almost permanent substitutes for public schools which failed to arrive. Sunday schools were cheap and boasted of a good record in providing basic literacy. As late as 1858 the American Union was still selling "hundreds of thousands" of its Spelling-Books across the nation. Sales were made to public schools but the bulk went to Sunday schools. One missionary in the South proudly reported knowing of one hundred persons who were taught the alphabet on Sundays in a period of eighteen months. Politicians in the West were sometimes tempted to let the Sunday schools, rather than public schools, serve the poor and sparsely settled neighborhoods or else by second-rate schools for immigrants. In Wisconsin, one Milwaukee delegate to the state constitutional convention of 1847 suggested that the foreign-born might learn English in the Sunday school since they often felt uncomfortable in the common schools. Though the money-saving gambit was rejected in Wisconsin, it remained a tempting option for others along the frontier.

Just as the western Sunday schools served multiple purposes, so did the missionaries sent out by the Union and the denominational societies. Often untrained and barely literate, these agents were sometimes the only educational "experts" known to local workers in the new states and territories. They never spent much time in any one place because the managers in the East wanted better statistics—more schools—rather than extensive care of established outposts. But at least they could leave behind "Sunday school libraries" which they were commissioned to sell. As the missionaries went from village to village, with the aid of a horse or a walking staff, they took catalogues of Union materials. The society went into book publishing in its first year, 1824–1825, when it offered alphabet primers, spelling books, hymnals, catechisms to suit nondenominational or denominational settings, Bibles and a wide variety of tracts or stories, most of which were lifted from English publications. For ten cents a copy, Hannah More's "The Shepherd of Salisbury Plain" was available, or for a total of 12½ cents both installments of "The Dairyman's Daughter (an authentic and Interesting Narrative)." The hymn book was $6 per 100, unless it was bound in sheepskin which raised the price to $14. Small reward tickets, in blue or red with a scripture text on each, were $1 per 1,000. "The Sunday School Teacher's Guide," by the Reverend J. A. James, abridged and revised by the Committee on Publications, 90 pages, was 14 cents.

At first the Union's Committee on Publication admitted to being *"dictators to the consciences of thousands of immortal beings."* Although that phrase was soon dropped from committee reports, members continued to be willing to become "responsible arbiters . . . rather than tamely issue sentiments which, in their consciences, they believe to be false, or inconsistent with the purity of divine truth."[14] In 1830 the committee condemned fiction as "silly stories, the very titles of which disgrace the annals of education." It approved of the "prodigious leap" from

Mother Goose's Melodies to Taylor's *Hymns for Infant Minds,* a better source of "intellectual and moral improvement."

Agents for the Sunday School Union had nothing less to do than "supply the whole youthful population of a country with rational and profitable books." One indication of substantial success in mid-nineteenth-century decades came in an 1859 *Manual of Public Libraries.* Out of more than 50,000 such libraries in the country, 30,000 were in Sunday schools, 18,000 in other schools and nearly 3,000 in city and town collections. That the Sunday school libraries were considered *public* is significant. In many places, especially villages and rural areas, these were the only sources of books available to any who could read.

The Sunday school movement managed to provide three-fifths of the American libraries by 1859 for at least three reasons. First, the Sunday School Union published inexpensive books. As an enthusiast said in 1831, the Union "gives a child a testament and teaches him to read for 37 cents." In the late 1830s the first "Sunday School and Family Library" was developed. The collection of "100 select volumes from 72 to 252 pages, substantially bound" sold for just $10. True, *The History of Robinson Crusoe* was missing but there was the story of a *Scottish Farmer,* a work on Bedouin Arabs and the tale of an *Affectionate Daughter-in-Law.*

Second, missionaries were under strict instructions not to leave a struggling new Sunday school without first selling it a library. If necessary, $5 could be offered out of funds supplied by eastern backers. The library was the true mark of a *bona fide* Sunday school. Finally, the libraries proved to be popular in many places. If immigrants from Protestant Europe decided to learn to read English, the Sunday school could furnish the practice texts. To those who came West from the eastern seaboard, the libraries signified learning and culture in an otherwise raw and brutish life far removed from "home." A rare Sunday school agent, such as John Adams, could "bring back recollections of a cultured Eastern home." But he always had to move on; meanwhile, the books remained as a visible and permanent reminder of a receding past.

The Union's editors in Philadelphia knew how to appeal to this nostalgia. Few of their publications were more revealing than

The Daisydingle Sunday-School, the story of what presumably happened in an Indiana wilderness town in the 1840s. In a crude village one little girl remembers her New England home and happy Sundays there. Her accounts awaken "vague hopes" in the hearts of other children. Arrives then an eastern relative who, finding no church or Sunday school, later sends "quite a nice library, of one hundred volumes . . . and some two or three dozen Testaments and Hymnbooks besides, which were all snugly packed in a box, and sent from Philadelphia by canal, steamboat, railroad, and wagon." "Daisydingle" had a big day when the box arrived, for it was a marvelous sight to see children "rejoice in the prospect of new books to read—story books with red or green backs and gilt letters, and pictures in them besides."[15]

This tale, a compound of sentiment, "sales pitch" and appeal for eastern money, also reflected the situation of many a wilderness area like "Daisydingle." Books were scarce, the Union had few competitors, and the Sunday school missionaries were usually the first visitors to settlements. They left a lasting imprint on the Middle West. Perhaps the most important contributions of these now forgotten educators were the omnipresent Sunday school libraries, whose tattered remains can still be unearthed in church basements.

Other Frontiers, Partly Explored

The Valley campaign was a considerable success despite several setbacks. An economic depression, the Panic of 1837, hit all the national benevolent societies. The Sunday School Union never fully recovered the enormity of its previous momentum but neither did it collapse. Denominational Sunday school societies took up the slack and the movement boomed in the Valley. By the eve of the Civil War the most promising younger leaders were in Illinois, where Stephen Paxson and others had labored so long. This shift of power from East to West, carrying out the predictions of the 1830s, became more evident after the North-South strife was over. The missionaries had done their work. Indeed, the success of the Valley campaign was so absorbing that it deflected serious attention from relative failure on two other frontiers that would be important and troubling in later years. One frontier was urban; the other was black America.

Particularly after 1840 a new situation was developing in eastern cities. The 1856 Sunday School Union report was straightforward in its abhorrence:

The refuse population of Europe, rolling in vast waves upon our shores, as it passes westward, deposits its dregs upon our seaboard. These congregate in our great cities and send forth their children—a wretched progeny, degraded in the deep degradation of their parents—to be the scavengers, physical and moral, of our streets. Mingled with these are also the offcast children of American debauchery, drunkenness, and vice. A class more dangerous to the community . . . can hardly be imagined. And how are they to be reached? The public school and the church are . . . of no avail.

The only answer, the Union concluded, was "mission Sunday schools," latter-day versions of the old charity schools or "ragged schools" and forerunners of the late nineteenth-century "institutional city churches" and settlement houses.

Intermittent attempts to establish mission Sunday schools in the cities took place from the 1850s on. But urban "destitute places" never seemed to deserve anything like the support lavished upon the western frontier. The pattern of default was encouraged partly because Sunday school planners, like many Protestants of that time, looked upon the city as the symbol and source of human corruption, a gloomy place compared to the glamorous western mission field. That is not to say cities lacked Sunday schools. In fact, enrollments were high, especially in Boston and New York, with greatest strength in the more settled and prosperous Anglo-Saxon sections. It was an early case of suburbs versus the inner city. The Protestant mindset against urbanization was deeply rooted and the expansive West with its courageous individuals looked ever so much more like a promised land.

The anti-Catholic sentiments of the 1850s also contributed to the slowness in setting up urban Sunday school missions. A distinct flavor of the "Native American" ideology showed through the Sunday School Union's references to "refuse" and "dregs." Frelinghuysen, in one of his last speeches to the Union, spoke bitterly of "the mighty tide of emigration flowing in upon our shores." The old man—the year was 1858—warned that "infidelity and priestcraft have joined hand in hand in unholy alliance to eradicate those ever-living principles of truth upon which the Puritans planted this government." A spirit of distaste and resentment was unwittingly communicated to the potential recipients of mission Sunday school benefits. Predictably, the charity schools were not well received by the poor, as they had not been earlier. Most workers retreated to more familiar baliwicks. After the Civil War the American Sunday School Union concentrated on the rural scene, while mainline denominations stayed close to their migrating middle-class constituencies. The tendency toward default on the urban frontier was characteristic of the movement by the end of the nineteenth century.

The national Sunday school movement's failure on the frontier of black America in pre-Civil War days was probably inevitable. Leaders were profoundly embarrassed by the "problem of the colored people" as they knew it through most of the nineteenth century. The whole black experience was a mystery which the Sunday School Union felt little compulsion to comprehend. Besides, the men launching the Valley campaign did not really expect to find black children in the destitute places of the West. As it turned out, some missionaries did work among black Americans, starting a fair number of "colored" schools and black classes within white schools. These makeshift arrangements were never celebrated or publicized "back East" as were safer, whiter exploits. The risk of giving much attention to a minority was too great.

Black denominations established before 1865 were not, significantly, waiting around for white help in educating their people. In the North the African Methodist Episcopal Church (started in 1787 in Philadelphia) and the African Methodist Episcopal Zion Church (emerging in New York in 1796) went ahead with the formation of schools on Sunday. The development was crucial, for it often provided the only available opportunity for learning. The first black Sunday school in the West was opened by an AME church in Chillicothe, Ohio, in 1829. The same denomination sponsored Sunday education in New England, Pennsylvania,

Maryland and Washington, D.C. early in the nineteenth century. In the period between 1830 and 1860, as one black Sunday school missionary put it, "the Sabbath school was made a necessary appendage of the Church." This parallelism of congregation and school followed the typical pattern of all denominational growth. The Sunday school, however, was much more than an appendage in some black communities; it was *the* school, without which there would have been no literacy training at all.

The story of the slave Sunday school in the South is enormously complex and approaches the grotesque. By 1835 all southern states had adopted reactionary legislation making the education of slaves illegal. South Carolina was first in 1740. The more punitive measures against literate slaves came in the early nineteenth century when anxiety over slave insurrections intensified. Actual observance of these laws varied considerably from plantation to plantation within a state during the first three decades of the century. The educational fate of a slave depended on the perspective of his owner. Some masters believed in literate slaves because reading and writing increased the efficiency of the labor force. Other sympathetic whites advocated education as a means of assisting an oppressed class. White missionaries frequently insisted upon teaching for the sake of the slaves' salvation. In all these instances the Sunday school was a natural instrument for realizing goals set by whites. Despite state laws, Sunday instruction flourished intermittently across the South in those years when the Protestant "benevolent empire" was shaping up. Sometimes concerned whites used oral instruction as a subterfuge to evade the intent of the antiliteracy laws.

As cotton became king and the plantation system grew more rigid, many planters experienced apprehension about educated slaves. They feared that the barest training in letters might disturb the peace of the contented field and house hands. Literate slaves who would have been prized property in the eighteenth century were "considered more dangerous than useful" as the nineteenth century progressed. Carter Woodson observed: "Doomed . . . to be half-fed, poorly clad, and driven to death in this cotton kingdom, what need had the slaves for education?"[16]

Slave rebellions of the 1830s added to a growing prejudice

against Sunday schools. It was known that Nat Turner's education was "chiefly acquired in the Sunday schools in which 'the text-books for the small children were the ordinary speller and reader, and that for the older Negroes the Bible.' "[17] Those planters who had ignored state prohibitions against teaching slaves were less inclined to do so when they saw Sunday classes as potential breeding grounds for revolution and trouble. In the 1830s oral instruction was strongly discouraged, if not stamped out, in most places. Slave teachers, who had not been unusual, were suppressed.

A few white people responded by arguing for strictly supervised schools run by white missionaries. They reiterated the claim that ignorance, even for slaves, was unproductive. Several denominations took part in a campaign to place white Sunday school workers among blacks. The goal was a *modestly* literate, *always* obedient slave. Charles C. Jones was one of the missionaries who labored among the slaves. In 1842 he wrote one of the first books on the history of black education in America. A well-intentioned man, Jones nevertheless presupposed a caste system and maintained that religious instruction did not produce insubordination. "The Gospel recognizes the condition in which the Negroes are," he wrote, "and inculcates the duties appropriate to it. Ministers are commanded by the Apostle Paul to 'exhort servants to be obedient to their own masters and to please them well in all things. . . .' "[18]

Missionary-run Sunday schools inculcating subservience were often satisfactory to the plantation whites. A South Carolina slaveowner reportedly said in the pre-Civil War period:

Some years ago my people were a very insubordinate people; it was very hard to get along with them, and the severest measures had to be used; but a few years ago missionary work was begun—the work of the catechism; preachers had to teach as we teach in the Sunday school; their instructions were largely catechetical; and now I go to sleep every night with the sound of the songs and prayers . . . ringing in my ears, and I have now no use for any of the measures that were used before.[19]

A most useful institution, the Sunday school, for some.

Just as the large Sunday school agencies never gave much

attention to the black population, they were usually silent on slavery itself and abolition. In this they were quite different from their British counterparts, for Sunday school forces in Great Britain were basically united in an attack on drink, war and slavery, the "trinity of evils" in the estimate of many evangelicals. The American movement focused almost entirely on the "curse of liquor." From its inception, the American Sunday School Union was friendly to the temperance cause and by the 1850s the saloon was commonly considered the "Sunday school of Satan." But the Union had little to say about war, and on slavery it maintained a sterile silence.

Lack of American opposition to slavery was mystifying and disturbing to some of the English brethren. Stephen Tyng, an Episcopal clergyman from Philadelphia, encountered rage when he spoke as the American Sunday School Union representative at the 1842 meeting of the Sunday School Union in London. Some members of his audience could not imagine how anyone could speak for an hour on American Sunday schools and never once allude to a mission to free the slaves.

As the conflict over slavery grew and the Civil War approached, the Sunday school leaders remained immobilized as a group. However, a fair number of scattered individuals were abolitionists and some Sunday schools supported the antislavery crusade. When a Sunday school superintendent from Oberlin, Ohio, was held two months without trial in Cleveland for work in the "underground railroad," the children of the Oberlin Sabbath School Association—400 of them—conducted in 1859 what may have been the first jail "sit-in." The youngsters went to Cleveland on the invitation of Plymouth Church's Sunday school and filled up the jail, considerably "enlivening" it. Four days after they went home their superintendent was released.

The Oberlin children's stand for the rights of the superintendent was, however, not characteristic of the "glory story" usually reported by the movement's magazines. The jail tale would have constituted a breach of the neutrality on controversial social matters—the stand of most other national Protestant societies. William Lloyd Garrison, kingpin of the Abolitionists, looked upon the "big name" organizations as equally culpable partners in a conspiracy of silence, a policy of complicity instead of neutrality. In 1855 Garrison proposed to the American Antislavery Society that it pass a resolution condemning many groups, including the Sunday School Union, as "being in league and fellowship with the slave-holders of the South, utterly dumb in regard to the slave system, and inflexibly hostile to the antislavery movement." He thought such organizations should be "instantly abandoned by every one claiming to be the friend of liberty and a disciple of Christ."[20]

Garrison's charges were resented but largely ignored. For years the evangelical societies had shied away from those wanting to convert them into antislavery units and would not deviate from a proven policy in the middle of the excruciating tensions of the 1850s. The Sunday School Union could not so much as publicly discuss the coming cataclysm without tearing itself apart. Popular, mass-based voluntary organizations always depend on a consensus that includes workers and donors of utterly different outlooks. To damage that consensus, or even to stretch it, was to risk institutional immolation. Sunday school fathers were not willing to take the risk, choosing rather to play it safe by acting officially as though the "peculiar institution" of slavery should not interfere with the work of their movement. The Sunday school stood impotent before the pervasive powers of the American caste system.

Failure in the cities and inability to face up to slavery's implications were to return later to haunt the institution as it sought to explore the changing meaning of the imperative, enunciated in 1830, "to establish a Sunday school in every destitute place."

CHAPTER III

From Death to Sunbeams: Songs and Stories of the Movement

You ask why I cannot keep my religion to myself? I will tell you, my dear brother. Because I see you are in danger of eternal damnation. [1]

—LEWIS TAPPAN

In their prime, American reform movements sing. Civil rights marchers of the mid-1960s had "We Shall Overcome" to hurl at hecklers and to draw them together. Earlier in the twentieth century the labor forces sang as they struck. One sure sign of labor's demise as a movement appeared when only the older union members could recall the verses of "Solidarity Forever." The Sunday school also sang. Knit together by common memories and even more by vivid expectations of a new future, the movement produced thousands of hymns and songs. The zeal captured in music and no less in stories, is both cause and result of the basic success of the Sunday school.

The best known of all its songs came out of a novel published in 1860. *Say and Seal* was written by two sisters, Anna and Susan Warner, who managed to teach West Point cadets on Sundays as well as to produce best-sellers. Not surprisingly, the plot pivots around the doings of several persons involved in a Sunday school. A sweet girl named Faith Derrick is beloved by John Linden, a devoted Sabbath teacher. Among the scholars is little Johnny Fax. The Warners refused to say whether the names "Faith" and "Fax (facts)" were contrived to juxtapose or just happened.

Central to the story of the triangle is young Johnny's declining health. Despite the ministrations of Miss Derrick and Linden, the boy seems destined to die. When Linden asks what he can do for the lad, Johnny holds up his bony arms to his teacher and says, "Walk—like last night." Linden picks up the feverish child and slowly walks back and forth and for a moment Johnny is quiet. Then he says, "Sing." Still rocking the frail creature in his arms, Linden begins a new song, one Johnny has not heard before. Faith hears every word clearly and distinctly:

> Jesus loves me, this I know, / For the Bible tells me so;
> Little ones to him belong, / They are weak but he is strong.
>
> Jesus loves me—he who died, / Heaven's gate to open wide;
> He will wash away my sin, / Let his little child come in.
>
> Jesus loves me, loves me still, / Though I'm very weak and ill;
> From his shining throne on high, / Comes to watch me where I lie.
>
> Jesus loves me—he will stay/Close beside me all the way,
> Then his little child will take/Up to heaven for his dear sake.

A few minutes later, before reading some of the boy's favorite verses from the book of Revelation, Linden turns to Faith and says, "We were permitted to show him the way at first, Faith, but he is showing it to us now." Johnny Fax dies.

The new song was set to music in 1861 by William B. Bradbury who added the chorus, "Yes Jesus loves me . . . the Bible tells me so." *Say and Seal* and the song, "Jesus Loves Me," came midway in the development of the Sunday school's faith. While the Warner sisters' tale pointed backward, the hymn pointed ahead. Despite the death-tinged lyrics, "Jesus Loves Me" was a sign of the future with its jaunty, cheerful jingle. It set a new style of Sunday school music, one of the songs friendly to people, with melodies that sang themselves and had plenty of "go." The "go" songs became popular in the years from 1860 to 1914 because they reflected an emerging *soft faith,* a more reassuring version of childhood and life's demands.

And so the song anticipated changing concepts. The novel, in contrast, contained many of the conventions found in a long line of Anglo-American religious literature, going back to English evangelical authors in the days of Robert Raikes. Central themes were the constant shadow of death, the importance of the Bible and the child as religious guide. Early nineteenth-century Sunday school books and their eighteenth-century predecessors demanded *hard faith,* a stern and somber vision of childhood and of all life.

Little Adults

If sex is the common preoccupation of Americans in the mid-twentieth century, then death was the obsession of evangelical Protestants in the first half of the nineteenth. Their stories teemed with dying people; Sunday school books moved toward the predictable, climactic death of a pious hero. Authors lavished such prurient attention on deathbed details that the accounts were almost obscene. Not that deathbed prose was anything new for devout Protestants of England or America. The generation of William Wilberforce and Hannah More was fascinated by the drama of ebbing life. Mrs. More found nothing so interesting, she wrote to a friend, "as the closing scenes of a champion of righteousness."[2] There were many "champions of righteousness" in the literature of the early Sunday school.

A popular title in the Union's first 100-volume library was *A Memorial for Sunday School Boys: being an Authentic Account of the Conversion, Experience, and Happy Deaths of Twelve Boys.* The companion volume for girls had thirteen stories! *A Memorial for Sunday School Boys* was a "reward book," a prize given to those who had memorized huge chunks of Scripture and/or attended regularly. Typical of one of these grisly rewards is the account of the "happy death" of William Quayle, age nine:

William Quayle was born October 21st, 1778. He seemed to have the fear of the Lord from his infancy, which produced in him a holy zeal for the glory of God. This he manifested by frequently reproving sinners, especially his mother; which reproofs, after she was deprived of him caused her much sorrow of heart, on account of her not having paid greater attention to them. He used also often to tell her that God would be angry with her if she did not turn from her evil ways. . . . He would also reprove wicked children . . . playing in the streets.

As soon as he was about three years old, he began to pray every night before he went to bed, which he would never do but on his knees.

He was also very tender hearted; for if his mother chastized any of his little brothers, he would frequently weep over them on account of their folly and suffering. In a word, he spent a life (short as it was) to the glory of God . . . but, if, through any accident or inattention he had done amiss, he would fall down on his knees, and ask pardon immediately.

He pitied the condition of the neighbouring children, because they would not walk in the fear of the Lord. . . . In September, 1787, he was seized with his last sickness, which continued about a fortnight.

When his father used to express his hope that he would recover, he always replied, "I would rather die than stay here." Though a child, he never complained of pain or sickness, but was patient and always resigned to the will of God.

A few minutes before he died, he cried out, "Father! Father! Mother! Mother! O my heaven! My heaven!" He then sung a hymn, and desired his mother to turn him in bed, and instantly fell asleep in the arms of his dear Redeemer, September 24, 1787, in the ninth year of his age.[3]

Happy deaths for saintly children were celebrated in many Sunday school songs. The 1835 hymnbook of the Sunday School Union offered suitable verses for the "Death of a Pious Child," "Death of a Scholar," "Triumph in Death" and "For a Dying Child." Number 275 was "The Fear of Death Removed," which assured the child that "Jesus can make a dying bed / Feel soft as downy pillows are." *Union Melodies* in 1838 added "The Grave." The fourth stanza contained these lines: "Then though the grassy bed, / The cold and gloomy cell, / Should bear my youthful head, / For me it will be well; / Yes, better far than dwelling here, / Away from home another year!" The stress on dying children in Sunday school song and story seems, at first glance, bloodchilling and perverse. Why this preoccupation with death? In part it reflected an old Protestant tradition, faithfully observed, and in part the reality of high mortality rates and population-thinning epidemics. Yet there are at least three other sources of equal importance.

1. *Death was not a forbidden topic in the late eighteenth and early nineteenth centuries.* Death was feared but could be dealt with openly in the world of evangelical Protestants because there were far greater terrors. More ominous was the prospect of God's righteous judgment. Sunday school workers disagreed on whether Judgment Day was immediate or temporarily postponed after death. But few disagreed about its inevitability and awe-provoking power. This dread and certainty found expression in the hymns which in the 1835 Sunday School Union book included "Judgment-day," "The Judge" and "The Wicked Child Judged." The last gave unrepentant youngsters a macabre image: "How dreadful, Lord, will be the day / When all the tribes of dead shall rise, / And those who dared to disobey, / Be brought before thy piercing eyes." The "terrors of that day"—a phrase from still another song—were more feared than death. Paradoxically, the terrors allowed a greater freedom in facing death.

2. *Real deathbed scenes were household, if not public, events in contrast to the modern cloistering of death in hospital privacy.* Death was an occasion for a family educational experience when "last words" were viewed as unusually illuminating and the manner of dying was closely observed. People near death were thought close to eternity, and reflections of heaven might be caught in their eyes. And the impact of death, especially that of a child, could inspire others to renew their Christian faith and thus prepare for the "terrors of that day."

3. *The most important single motive for the relentless evangelical emphasis on dying children was that preoccupation with death threw the desperate urgency of life into bold relief.* Obviously a scare tactic, a strong weapon for pushing people toward "right" action and "true belief," this emphasis was also an affirmation of life, a breakthrough in concepts of the possibilities of childhood. As late as the eighteenth century some religious people acted as though children did not exist. Philippe Ariès has explained, in his brilliant history of family life, why children were often neither heard nor seen. He tells of consolation offered to a seventeenth-century woman after a birth made

her "the mother of five 'little brats.' " A neighbor assured her that, "Before they are old enough to bother you, you will have lost half of them, or perhaps all of them." Cruel? Perhaps, by modern standards, but, as Ariès concludes, people in former centuries could not "allow themselves to become too attached to something that was regarded as a probable loss . . . . Nobody thought, as we ordinarily think today, that every child already contained a man's personality. Too many of them died."[4] Indifference can offer protection against crippling loss.

Then along the way in the eighteenth century a shift of monumental importance long in the making, became evident. The first generation of Sunday school champions—like Robert Raikes noticing factory children running rampant on Sundays—took part in the culturally revolutionary discovery of the child. Only the "child" they had in mind was a little adult, utterly different from the popular image held today. Portrayals of children in Sunday school material as late as the 1880s presented miniature adults, like elders in dress, stance, gesture—in everything except size. The similarity did not stop there. An evangelical child was no innocent lamb. His early and deep complicity in the kingdom of Satan and sin was taken for granted; death was not alien and mortality was omnipresent. Life could be compressed into a few years and death a constant companion. The "William Quayles" and "Johnny Faxs," had to live faster and better than the Sunday school equivalents of "Dick and Jane and their dog, Spot" in the mid-twentieth century. In the modern juvenile world death occasionally afflicts animals—a pet, maybe loyal "Spot"—but seldom a human being.

The fast-developing, death-approaching children of the early nineteenth century were capable of considerable accomplishments, particularly in their religious tutelage of adults. Johnny Fax and William Quayle held no monopoly on guidesmanship. A perennial and often varying tale concerns the town drunkard who is wooed back to sobriety and faith by his son, ably aided by the whole Sunday school. Child-sized religious virtuosos could convert servants, parents, older relatives, friends, hardhearted benefactors and strangers. Nobody apparently questioned the credibility of a remarkable little adult who appeared in the first

Sunday school book published in America. *Little Henry and His Bearer* was a "reward book" like *A Memorial for Sunday School Boys*. At eight and one-half years of age Henry could read the Bible in two languages, conduct learned arguments about the Christian faith, cite Scripture appropriately in diverse situations and ably assist others toward conversion.

An intense purposefulness and a resolute single-mindedness marked these model children. Not a minute could be wasted on games, play, laughter, the sports of the frivolous and self-indulgent "Tom Trifles." The pleasures of childhood, or pleasures of any kind, were infrequently mentioned at Sunday school. A hymn based on Matthew 16:24 stated it well: "Perish earthly fame and treasure, / Come disaster, scorn and pain; / In thy service pain is pleasure— / With thy favor life is gain." This is not Horatio Alger speaking. The Sunday school heroes were uninterested in being tycoons, or in the comforts of fame, money and prominence. Although they were dutiful and reliable in their chores, they kept their eyes on the one goal worthy of evangelical anxiety and energy—the double accomplishment of repentance of sin and conversion to God's purpose. Conversion was the moment of truth, *the* decision about the future, *the* choice between perpetual punishment and eternal peace. Heaven and hell were the only future alternatives and the choice was, finally, up to each individual. Other matters such as wealth and privilege faded in comparison with the prospect of a heavenly home. *The Union Spelling Book* of 1838 summed up the sentiment in verse: "It signifies not what our stations have been, / Nor whether we're little or great; / For happiness lies in the temper within, / And not in the outward estate." The pressure for conversion hit both real and "little adults" laboring to measure up to a hard faith.

A Religion of the Heart

Rigorous religion—hard faith—had some virtues suiting it to the frontier's hard times. Indeed, the somber vision of life corresponded to many realities prevailing in East as well as West. It took "little adults" to endure the short, harsh life of childhood, to remain sane through loneliness, disruption and death. The early Sunday school's faith was uncluttered, a simple gospel for plain folks on the move, requiring none of the elaborate doctrinal apparatus of classical Puritan thought and life. A tough-minded confidence about personal destiny was needed and, hopefully, loyal Sunday school members would continue to fight no matter what the odds. Teachers, who were expected to whet the desire for assurance, had their models; one was General Oliver O. Howard, who said to his troops before facing the Confederates: "I am going to lead you in a few days against the enemy; what will be the result of the battles I know not, nor how many of you will come out alive I cannot tell; Oh, if I knew every one of you were saved for God, how differently would I marshal you against the enemy."[5]

Although this sort of untrammeled confidence encouraged fanaticism and absolutism (the corruption of hard faith), it did provide a needed source of energy and an indifference to hazards and uncertainties. The strict outlook, above all, suggested a clear mandate for the Sunday school. Its real business—at least in the estimate of many leaders in the movement—was to be an incubator for the conversion of the young. Nothing else finally mattered. To "save souls," to be a "Teacher in the Sabbath school"[6] was more important, wrote Lewis Tappan to his brother, than being a United States Senator. This concern drove the Sunday school to become a how-to-do-it movement for conversion and made it a natural ally of the revival system pervading nineteenth-century American Protestantism.

Revivalism and the Sunday school had much in common. They tended to read the future in the same stripped-down either/or fashion. They grew simultaneously, shared enemies and embraced religion as an affair of the heart. A degree of cold logic is detected in the way story writers presented "little adults" capable of persuasive reasoning, but the purpose and impact were emotional. The involvement of the heart, especially in conversion, was essential to evangelicals, decidedly so in the opinion of Charles Finney, the leading revivalist of the mid-nineteenth century. "Finney's basic theorem," historian Perry Miller has noted, "was that everybody can agree upon intellectual propositions.

The difference is that some grasp them with the heart, others with only the mind."[7] Actually that "theorem" was "basic" for most evangelical Protestants, whether they were leading a revival or teaching a class on Sunday. The Sunday school movement used the distinction between heart and mind to draw a line between its work and any other institution—for example, the public school. To solve a mathematical equation or to study Shakespeare, according to one leader, was "a mere mental gymnastic." But the Sunday school was unique because its fruits included "practical truth."[8] What could be more practical than choosing the right destiny? Since the language and logic of Sunday school was "of the heart" the intellect had to take second place.

The mosaic of "hard faith" contained the coming Judgment Day, children as "little adults," man's two alternative futures, the separation of "heart" from "mind," and a conversion-conscious Sunday school mission. All this was part of the conventional wisdom when the Warner sisters wrote *Say and Seal,* launching "Jesus Loves Me." If an explanation of why these things were believed had been requested, Sunday school advocates might well have answered with the song's punchline, "The Bible tells me so." But the Bible was going to tell other stories in post-Civil War America.

The Growth of Innocence

The years following the War brought about subtle changes, barely perceptible at the time, in the Sunday school faith. Familiar symbols and forms were still the vogue. Robert Raikes was the most beloved and the "old-time religion" of the heart seemed good enough for generations to come. However, what the heart required was different in industrial America.

Nowhere is the contrast between the Sunday school in the early and the late nineteenth century more obvious than in its songs. Indicative of change are lyrics about the Sunday school itself. "The Sabbath School" in the 1838 *Union Melodies* stressed punctuality, obedience and solemnity. An ethos of dour earnestness prevailed, as the two stanzas show:

To Sabbath-school, to Sabbath-school, / We'll haste, we'll haste away;
We'll early be at Sabbath-school, / Nor ever stop to play.

At Sabbath-school, at Sabbath-school, / This precious holy day,
We'll careful be at Sabbath-school, / Our lessons well to say.

Fifty years or so later the corresponding song was "The Sunday School Brigade," whose dominant themes were zesty marching, joy, sunshine and "endless day":

Hear the tramp, tramp, tramp of the Sunday-School Brigade,
    Whether rain or shine we are always on parade;
By our Savior led, in the sunshine of His love,
    We are marching on to the land of joy above.

Hear the tramp, tramp, tramp of the Sunday-School Brigade,
    We would win that crown which will never, never fade;
We will trust our King, whersoever be the way,
    We will follow Him to the realm of endless day.

These verses reflect at least two transitions overtaking the "brigade's" music in the second part of the nineteenth century; dourness gave way to hearty, victory songs bristling with military metaphors, and the terrors of judgment day were mitigated.

The impact of the Civil War on Sunday school music is undeniable. The military image and the cavalry cadence resounded in "We are in the Saviour's Army," "I Am a Little Soldier" and "Hold the Fort" (more popular in the North than in the South since it was based on an episode out of General Sherman's march through Georgia.) "Hold the Fort" was the type of song with "go":

Ho, my comrades! see the signal waving in the sky!
Reinforcements now appearing, victory is nigh.
"Hold the fort, for I am coming," Jesus signals still;
Wave the answer back to heaven, "By thy grace we will."

The line, "We will follow Him to the realm of endless day" in the "Sunday School Brigade" is perhaps even more indicative of a shifting emphasis than the march tempo. Very few of the post-Civil War Sunday school hymns echoed the grim warnings of

Judgment Day. The mournful "Death of the Pious Child" of the 1830s was replaced by the upbeat "There's a Great Day Coming." Two alternative futures were still in style, but what a difference! Evangelicals of an earlier day could never have spoken of the final disclosure of divine wrath as a "great day." The nearer the twentieth century came, the more the Sunday school's songs of judgment sounded like descriptions of a family reunion. Hell was no longer overwhelming in its terrors. The individual's religious worry, explicated in song, swirled around the fear that God might somehow overlook him when passing out heaven-bound tickets. Immortality was the great reward to be claimed and divine forgetfulness was more threatening than divine wrath.

"Shall we Gather at the River?" spoke directly to the possibility of divine carelessness. With words and tune by the Reverend Robert Lowry, who composed the music for "I Need Thee Every Hour" and "We're Marching to Zion," this hymn first came to national prominence when thousands of youngsters marched through the streets of Brooklyn ("The City of Sunday Schools") in the 1865 Sunday school parade, singing these words:

Shall we gather at the river, / Where bright angel feet have trod;
With its crystal tide forever / Flowing by the throne of God?

Yes, we'll gather at the river, / The beautiful, the beautiful river;
Gather with the saints at the river / That flows by the throne of God.

The reassurance of that "yes" struck home and Lowry's hymn was followed by countless others along the same line. They ranged from the soft, caressing, maternal touch of Fanny Crosby's "Safe in the Arms of Jesus" to the hard-driving aggressiveness of Charlie D. Tillman's "Life's Railway to Heaven," the epitome of the rollicking, almost rolling revival music thatthat swept the Sunday school. And no wonder. Its assurance of heaven and its emphasis on speed, effort and human autonomy meshed nicely with the sense of life in a country undergoing the throes of industrialization. In the first verse came the challenge:

Life is like a mountain railroad, / With an engineer that's brave;
We must make the run successful, / From the cradle to the grave;

Watch the curves, the fills, the tunnels; / Never falter, never quail;
Keep your hand upon the throttle, / And your eye upon the rail.

Then the reward:

As you roll across the trestle, / Spanning Jordan's swelling tide,
You behold the Union Depot / Into which your train will glide;
There you'll meet the Sup'rintendent, / God the Father, God the Son,
With the hearty, joyous plaudit, / "Weary pilgrim, welcome home."

John Bunyan's pilgrim had come a long way; God was confined
to waiting in a heavenly depot for the arrival of man, who was
the center of activity and power. This was Calvinism totally
unstrung; "salvation" and immortality had become an achieve-
ment rather than a gift. God's sovereignty went, as by subversion,
into the shadows.

As the hopeful word about the divine plaudits awaiting pil-
grims at the end was voiced abroad, Sunday school leaders were
also confidently discovering new and better ways to begin the
"run successful." The "little adults" of stories and songs from
pre-Civil War days were increasingly irrelevant. A handful
mourned the dwindling popularity of "Little Henry" and his
friends, but many Protestants looked upon the older literature as
dull books about unbelievably good children who suffer a premature death. Off to the basements went the Sunday School Union
Library Number 1 with its pious children too good to live. A
modern, *natural* image of childhood was emerging.

The same revolt occurred in the realm of church music. By the
turn of the century the death music of the old-time Sunday
school had acquired a dismal reputation. Such songs as "The
Grave" and "Death of a Pious Child" were dismissed by the disdainful epithet, "mortuary hymns." The strongest critic of these
songs was the "religious education" movement of the early twentieth century, a group of reformers sensitive to the promptings
of progressive theories of John Dewey and other liberals. One
incipient reformer condemned mortuary hymns as "unfitted for
childhood" and suggested that such lines as "Hold thou the cross
before my closing eyes, / Shine through the gloom and point me
to the skies" were for more mature years. "No healthy, happy
child desires to die," he continued. "Sunday school hymnology

should exhale a natural, healthy sentiment. It should delight in nature, in God, in Christ, in home and country, and cherish the larger love of mankind. It should be cheerful and joyous like childhood itself, but always chaste, reverent and devotional." He labeled as "false sentiment" the verse blessing Sunday school as that place a "child of grace" would rather stay than spend his hours in play.[9]

These swift and decisive judgments about natural and false sentiment reflected fundamental upheavals taking place at the root of American culture during the presidencies of William McKinley, Theodore Roosevelt and William Howard Taft. It is at the level of what is taken for granted—the obvious, automatic truths—that the most radical changes in societies and nations occur and can be studied. The alert Sunday school leader, from the outset of the twentieth century, could begin to take for granted a different sense of time from that of his predecessor a few generations earlier. One source of this shift in attitude was the improvement in sanitation and ways of controlling disease. A progressive concept of natural childhood presupposed, or even anticipated, a lower rate of mortality. There was time to spare, time to enjoy the pleasures and advantages of a prelude to adulthood. The modern child had breathing space, a freedom from the onslaught of maturity and the distant rumor of death. Work, adulthood, the worries of the world—all these would come soon enough. For a few years at least, the American youngster should enjoy the temporary grace of childhood.

Not all Sunday school workers would have explicitly affirmed the virginal innocence of children. That would have been too abrupt and decisive a break with inherited theological tradition. Yet even the staunchest defender of the doctrine of original sin was affected by the emerging concept of childhood. While orthodox churchmen and the "religious educators" quarreled bitterly in the first decades of the twentieth century, they were united in one crucial respect: both embraced, though in varying degrees, the common ideal of the child as "sunbeam," a notion largely foreign to their evangelical ancestors.

It was an important agreement, for the rise of the "sunbeam" theme in the latter part of the nineteenth century represented a shift in the movement's perception of the child and his relation to nature.

Before the Civil War the Sunday school encouraged scholars to observe the moral character of nature. Nature told children to be industrious, sober and diligent in all things assigned by adults. *An Easy Introduction to the Knowledge of Nature* invited young readers to contemplate the spider, a mentor teaching "little boys and girls . . . both industry and exactness: for their webs are woven with the most perfect regularity." Bees were likewise edifying, since "the young ones learn readily what the old ones show them how to do; and little boys and girls should likewise be desirous of improving from the instructions that are given them."[10]

Different lessons were learned from nature in Sunday schools of the late nineteenth and twentieth centuries. Busy bees and industrious spiders were not entirely forgotten, but the new focus was on nature's beauty, its lovely and playfully delicate ways of expressing life. The carefree, trusting bird told an anxious child that "God is love, God is love, In his tender care, / Safe we rest, safe we rest, He is ev'rywhere."[11] And the flowers said, "God is love, joyfully children sing, / Tell all the glad story of your King."[12] In the song, "God is Everywhere," children were directed to breezes, shadows, sunlight, trees, flowers, birds and to their own hearts for signs of deity.[13]

In such profusion of beauty, the moral imperative of the Sunday school was for a child *to be* rather than *to do*. A life was like a simple sunbeam, a ray of light breaking through dark clouds to brighten the landscape. The Sunday schools became virtual classrooms for sunbeams. A variety of sunbeam songs have been located. One example, "I Will Be a Sunbeam," suffices:

> I will be a sunbeam ev'ry day, / Shining, tho' the skies are drear;
> Bringing golden sunshine all the way, / Speaking loving words of cheer.
> Sunbeams, sunbeams, / Shining for the Saviour far and near;
> Bringing golden sunshine all the way, / Speaking loving words of cheer.[14]

Sunbeam songs were so commonplace and sometimes so caricatured, that the intended meaning of their creators is hard to discover. Precise origins are also elusive. One of the first appearances of the sunbeam theme in Sunday school literature was in a story, *The Cloud and the Sunbeam,* written by Nellie Grahame and published by the Presbyterians in 1865. The moral was stated: "Bright, smiling faces, and looks of love sometimes brighten even the cares and sorrows of a home, and chase them all away." The narrative centered on a sunbeam who "once came to a saddened home in the shape of a little baby girl [Grace Stanley], with soft, brown eyes, and such a dear, little innocent face that no one could look upon it without loving it."[15] Little Grace became an even purer ray after her conversion. Later in the nineteenth century Nellie Grahame's cautionary note on conversion faded somewhat as *the child as the sunbeam* came into its own as a virtual Sunday school doctrine. Grace Stanley and her successors were persuasive precisely because they were different from mature people, anything but "little adults." The carefree, playful, trusting and dependent sunbeam cast the momentary light of innocence upon an otherwise soiled and troubled world. Sunbeam children may have been created as much to provide momentary escape for Sunday school workers raised under the symbols of hard faith as they were to explain childhood to children.

Bird, flower and sunbeam songs, when taken together, constituted a striking testament of faith in the beneficence of nature. The birds were always happy, breezes gentle and flowers blooming and nodding in the warm sun of a peaceful, serene kingdom. This dreamy, serpentless garden of Eden in the Sunday school outlook is all the more remarkable in light of the religious and cultural anxiety stirred up in late nineteenth-century America by Charles Darwin's *On the Origin of Species* and the debate over the survival of the fittest. If the writers of children's hymns shared Alfred Tennyson's lament about nature "red in tooth and claw," they seldom revealed it. Their prevailing desire was probably to protect children—regardless of how and where the species originated—from the darker side of life and thus preserve innocence as long as possible. The result, whatever the motive, was an incorrigibly sentimental appraisal of childhood and nature.

Sentimentality is the corrupter of any soft faith just as fanaticism and absolutism despoil hard faith. A corrupted sentiment was present, for instance, in the hymn writers' concern for unfortunate children, whether near or far away. Should a local mischief-maker steal a quince or apple, a sunbeam was obliged, as one song put it, to "Tell him to halt! tell him to halt! / Whatever may be his fault."[16] More often, the unfortunate and needy children were overseas, as was "The Little Hindoo Girl":

> I am a little Hindoo girl, / Of Jesus never heard;
>   Oh, pity me, dear Christian child, / Oh, send to me His word.
> Oh, pity me, for I have grief / So great I cannot tell,
>   And say if truly there's a heaven, / Where such as I can dwell.

The next verse tells how the "dear Christian child" is speeding the gospel around the globe and will eventually be glad to greet the "little Hindoo girl" before the heavenly throne. Zeal for the ultimate joy of the needy was one response. A sunbeam child could also give practical help to the unfortunate with only a penny, "Not on apples or cakes, or playthings to spend it, / But over the seas to the heathen to send it."[17]

These sentimental songs were attuned to the aspirations and needs of the day in American Protestant culture. Hard faith may have given way to soft faith but religion was still very much an affair of the heart. Moreover, it was the era of the expanding Protestant empire, a time when the mission network circled the globe and people of many lands joined Britishers and Americans in the cry, "Lift up the cross of Jesus, / His banner be unfurled, / Till every tongue confess Him through / The whole wide world."

Sunday schools were being planted on every continent; children in African rain forests, Australian deserts and Alaskan igloos soon had their own versions of "Sunbeams for Jesus" and "Shall We Gather at the River?" None of the songs, however, was more universally adopted than "Jesus Loves Me." Translated into countless languages and dialects—including Hindustani for the "little Hindoo girl"—the poem of the Warner sisters became the alma mater of the Sunday school movement. Doubtless each culture assigned its own meaning to the words. That was fair enough. American Protestants claimed scriptural sanction for their conviction about "Life's Railway to Heaven" and the pure innocence of children. Other nationalities in quite different circumstances could just as legitimately fit their cultural and religious values under the generous canopy of that ever-popular phrase, "this I know, For the Bible tells me so."

CHAPTER IV

A Pinch of Harvard,
A Heap of Tammany Hall

*God skimmed the church and poured the cream
into the Sunday school.*

—WILLIAM REYNOLDS

The Sunday school movement experienced a "second birth" after the Civil War. Progress from death songs to sunbeams and from children as "little adults" to innocents was involved, but these shifts were partly cultural inevitabilities. The transformation of the Sunday school into *the* worldwide work of evangelical Protestantism was quite deliberately and thoroughly the work of an energetic group of men—the "Illinois Band."

A Northern army camp in 1864 was the setting for the first encounter in the remarkable collaboration which baptized boosterism, almost deified organization and sent "the Army of the Lord" marching toward the twentieth century. Dwight L. Moody, Chicago salesman turned full-time evangelist, and William Reynolds, a Peoria businessman, were doing civilian religious work among the troops. They were, on one occasion, discussing the future. In Reynolds' often told and probably later embellished recollection, Moody proposed that they go into Sunday school activity when the war ended since "teaching the children of this country the way to Christ and then building them up in Christ" was the "greatest work in this world." The evangelist told Reynolds to go to Springfield the next June for a state Sunday school convention. "Let us try to capture that convention and try to make it a power in the State," said Moody.[1] The convention was captured; a power was made in Illinois, and then in most of North America.

Included in the "Illinois Band" were Benjamin F. Jacobs, Baptist layman and produce dealer and later a real estate man in Chicago; John H. Vincent, a young Methodist clergyman; Edward Eggleston, a Sunday school editor and future author of *The Hoosier Schoolmaster;* Reynolds, and a host of lesser lights. Moody went on to bigger things as the leading revivalist of the Anglo-American world, while Jacobs and Vincent became a creative duo, partners in propelling the Sunday school movement for thirty years. These two were unequaled in genius for organization and an ability to attract other potential leaders. They had a flair for educational innovations, some of which have lasted to the present.

Men of a rising generation of evangelical organizers, the "Illinois Band" eventually found ready colleagues in such individuals as John Wanamaker, the enterprising Philadelphia merchant, and H. J. Heinz, of "57 varieties." These men shared striking similarities in background, experience and expectations. Most left home early to work in the cities, and their only college was the proverbial "school of hard knocks." Despite their disregard for the findings of Darwin, Jacobs and many of his cohorts had personally experienced the "survival of the fittest." Cities usually rewarded the aggressive and ambitious recruits, the go-getters who willingly endured long and hard hours; there was no romance in being second best.

A booster spirit was infecting people and cities, particularly in Chicago. One slightly envious Cincinnati resident noted that the Windy City was built on a "wet and miserable" marsh and "made a most beautiful city by pure enthusiasm." The same commentator found a parallel between the great amount of Sunday school work in Chicago and the amount of talk, adding, "But I glory in their talk; if they did not talk so much they would not work so much."[2] When a city—any city—dubbed itself "the most up-and-coming" in the "greatest state of the Union," Sunday school workers could hardly escape the chamber of commerce outlook, making their cause the "greatest in the world" and themselves the true avant-grade for the whole movement.

The new Sunday school organizers were touched by the urban revivals of the 1850s and accepted, without taint of reservation, the mid-nineteenth-century version of evangelical faith, complete with literal interpretation of the Bible and the second coming of Christ. All except Vincent, who was interested in theological study, were rather indifferent to intellectual issues of the day. Their real interest was elsewhere. They found the problems of organization intriguing and fascinating. Jacobs, Wanamaker and friends took aesthetic delight in transforming an inchoate mass of men and resources into a cleanly developed, purposeful institution. To organize was not just a necessity; it was also the major creative act of life.

Their passion for order must be seen against the post-Civil War background when the country was caught up in the Gilded Age's accelerating process of change. In one historian's description,

The struggle to organize national life in new patterns, and the search for a viable collective identity ran all through the era's dynamic growth. ... What economic system could deal equally with a Pacific Coast facing the Orient, an Atlantic Coast competing with Europe, and a Gulf Coast looking toward South America? What did wool producers in Wyoming share with heavily industrialized Pennsylvania or New Jersey? Could a New Yorker understand the full meaning of a California orange that crossed a half-empty continent on a new railroad?[3]

The Sunday school movement, as well as denominations and their education societies, had been split by the war. How would reunion be accomplished? It helped, of course, that none of the prominent northern Sunday school men embraced the abolitionist cause or the "extremism" of John Brown. And after the war they stayed clear of Reconstruction controversies and debates over the rights of freedmen in the South. But there were belliger-

ent memories and the ghosts of dead loved ones from Gettysburg
and Chickamauga. Even among genial co-workers in the great
Sunday school cause, reunion was difficult.

East-West relations were edgy; the raw boastfulness of the
midwestern Sunday school associations did not quite conceal an
unspoken resentment against established, complacent ways in
the East. Further, considerable differences existed between rural
and urban schools. What did workers in sod huts in Kansas have
in common with the staffs of mammoth downtown churches in
Pittsburgh?

Such questions and uncertainties were unanswered in the late
1860s, yet by the 1890s the evangelical organizers had forged a
North American entity out of contradictory impulses and expectations. They were proud of the creation; so proud in fact that one
managed, in the course of a single speech, to compare the International Sunday School Convention—built by the "Illinois Band"
—to the educational reach of Harvard University and the organizational prowess of Tammany Hall, that erstwhile and infamous
Democratic machine in New York City. William Randolph, temporary chairman of the 1896 convention, rated his movement
ahead of Harvard but slightly behind that "wonderful organization called Tammany, which I have heard compared with the
Sunday-school Association."

Randolph's salute was surely no political endorsement, for almost to a man the northern Sunday school leaders in the late
nineteenth century leaned toward the Republican Party. (A Congregational minister quipped in 1871 that he had known "but one
Sabbath-school man who was a Democrat."[4]) The tribute was
that paid by an evangelical organizer to the true professionals in
the organizing enterprise. Randolph went on to explain how
Tammany divided New York City into districts, each with reliable contacts, so that any "voter that has to be interviewed" could
be reached without fail in twenty-four hours. The Sunday school
ideal was similar, said Randolph, and, if perfected, B. F. Jacobs
could "put upon the track of a sinner anywhere in this broad land
a Christian worker to speak to him of Christ." The emergence of
the Tammany model is the real story of the Sunday school convention system.

The Army of the Lord

National Sunday school conventions in the years 1869 to 1914 were somewhat like the quadrennial meetings of the Republicans and Democrats, except there was more lemonade than liquor consumed and not so much overt political conflict. The rise and fall of ambitious men was perhaps more obvious in the party conclaves, while women could vote and take part in Sunday school deliberations. Otherwise the triennial gatherings of the International Sunday School Convention—actually made up of workers from the United States and Canada—were genteel versions of the tribal festivities of politics—spectacles for the pretelevision age, replete with parades, slogans, public rallies, caucuses, musical numbers, group singing and, inevitably, more than enough oratory. The head of each state delegation reported on Sunday school activities, often beginning by praising the beauty of his state, the virtues of its citizens, and the splendor of its Sunday schools. "I have been gratified," said the New Jersey spokesman at the 1890 convention, "at hearing so many of you today tell us that you have the 'best' organization. There are forty-two [the number of states represented] 'best' organizations, and good speakers. I am glad you have them, for we in New Jersey make them and send them out to you."

The booster spirit of these occasions was not just innocent fun. The psychology of "quick growth and high hopes,"[5] the two ingredients in one definition of "boosterism," inspired the swift expansion of the Sunday school movement in the Gilded Age. Quick growth was a fact. After Moody, Jacobs and company captured the Illinois state convention in the 1860s, they discovered the absence of an effective national organization. The American Sunday School Union seemed old and sclerotic, enfeebled by financial troubles and staid programs. The "Illinois Band," along with some easterners, began to push for a nationwide convention system, a series of interconnected annual county and state meetings, with a national event every three years. The makings were all available in embryonic form. Sporadic county and state meetings were held before the Civil War, but the three early national

conventions—the 1832 gathering presided over by Theodore Frelinghuysen, an ill-advised, smaller one in 1833 and the 1859 convention in Newark—had done little to give coherence to the
system. Evangelical organizers vowed things would be different
after the fourth national meeting in 1869, and so they were.

By the time of the "First International Sunday School Convention" in 1875, a scant decade after the "Illinois Band" decided to
flex its muscles, the Army of the Lord had reassuring signs that
it was getting ready to move. Conventioneers could afford the
luxury of the ambitious word "international," for in 1875 a tiny,
though official, Canadian delegation attended. The ratio was
about twenty-three U.S. delegates for every Canadian! Perhaps a
more important symbolic occurrence at the 1875 convention was
an unofficial session of the Georgia and South Carolina delegates
with their counterparts from Massachusetts "to exchange hearty
Christian congratulations." As one Georgian said afterward to
the whole convention, "Down in the South, [Massachusetts] has
been regarded as a little bigoted and fanatical." He went on to
promise, after the laughter died down, that if his old enemies
from the Bay State remained true to the Sunday school, then he
could say, "God bless Massachusetts!" Given the hard feelings
engendered by the Civil War and Reconstruction, this was an
event of almost international significance. The evangelical organizers had proved to be adept diplomats.

The "Illinois Band" could be justly proud of their new organization that spanned the North American continent. With scarcely
any staff or full-time professional workers, they had developed
a voluntary network in most states and Canadian provinces.
Soon, they hoped, every township or county would have an annual convention reporting to yearly state assemblies. Thus the
triennial national convention would become the nerve center,
the heart of a system of communications in which anyone could
participate somewhere along the line. The something-for-every-
body approach provided the drama and excitement of a mass
movement, inspiration and encouragement for teachers, as well
as trips for pastors and Sunday school superintendents, and
plenty of room for amateurs. Clergy, it should be noted, did not
always dominate the proceedings. Here, as nowhere else except

the "Y" organizations, Protestant laymen were free from the hobbling constraints of second-class citizenship; they could break loose and exercise decisive leadership in a way seldom welcomed in denominational circles.

Sometimes the Sunday school convention provided a glimpse of a larger church, a more inclusive Christian community that could erase, if only for a few hours or days, the boundaries that walled off evangelical Christians from each other in ordinary parish life. At the 1902 gathering John Potts of Canada summed up twenty-five years of personal experience by describing the Sunday school as "the great 'evangelical alliance' which proves the unity, the spiritual unity, of evangelical Christianity."

Another virtue not often celebrated but nevertheless important was the relatively low cost of running the convention system, which required no sprawling bureaucracies or massive budgets. The convention fathers were fond of recommending the Sunday school as the most economical school in sight: "A minimum of expense, a maximum of benefit," a dictum applying also to the larger system. It was a tidy, thriving operation, an ingenious creation worthy of respect from Tammany Hall strategists.

Yet a big "if " loomed in the future. The convention network could expand as long as a mass of volunteers entertained high hopes. If those thousands of teachers, superintendents and loyal conventiongoers ever wavered in affection, the system was in trouble. The Sunday school movement was, like Chicago, "made . . . by pure enthusiasm" and the organizers were fully aware of this reality, although they could never be too explicit about it. From the 1860s on, a variety of methods was employed to keep the movement growing quickly and filled with high hopes. Most important was an appeal to the Gospel and the spirit of sacrifice and commitment. Then there was pride in home territories, that is, the desire to be a "banner" county or state convention and the stress on the civic function and responsibility of the Sunday school. The "numbers game" was no game to those Victorian Christians. The reassurance of statistical growth was helpful in the care and nurture of volunteers' morale. One of the first staff members of the International Convention was a statistical secretary, the chronicler of growth. His triennial report, an awesomely dull recital of facts, was among the most anticipated highlights of the conventions.

None of these tactics alone, however, would have sustained the momentum needed to keep the convention system operating. It was the foresight of B. F. Jacobs that kept the movement from floundering in the 1880s and 1890s. In the late 1860s the wily generalissimo of the "U. S. Sunday School Army" was preparing another gambit, an idea so simple and fascinating to his co-workers that it became the most talked about innovation in Protestant education since Robert Raikes opened his school for ragged children in Sooty Alley.

A Second Birth

Jacobs' coup was born out of a search for unity and a horror of inefficiency. The "Illinois Band," like many northerners after the Civil War, were enamored of the mystical notion of "Union." It was a natural romance. People were weary of war and had a distaste for any difference that might breed further conflict. Besides, the "Union" had been President Lincoln's guiding star, his principal article of faith, and if the Boys in Blue had fought and died for this cause, then the Sunday school workers could at least attempt to translate its meaning into civic and religious life. But what did "Union" mean? The elusive concept evoked quite different responses. To the practical-minded—who have counterparts in most postwar periods—it suggested the ideal of *uniformity;* uniformity of thought and action, they believed, would create a deeper *unity.*

The imperative of uniformity was doubly alluring to the rising generation of Sunday school leaders, particularly John H. Vincent. As a young pastor in the 1850s, he was appalled by the lack of order and system in the average Sunday school. Teachers could follow their own whims in choosing lesson materials; no common standards governed the recruitment or training of teachers. The result was a state of casual chaos. Methodist Bishop Francis J. McConnell recalled that his memory of Sunday morning in a pre-Vincent childhood was, " 'Johnny, read the first verse, Jimmy the second' and so on down to the little fellow who

could barely read. 'Have you any questions?' Nobody had. Then
tears would come into the teacher's eyes because we didn't seem
interested. Then came the collection box, into which we each
cast a cent."[6] This condition provoked Vincent into reforms in
teaching. If nothing else, the church could take cues from the
public school and have faculty meetings and regional normal
schools for training teachers.

Vincent started "Sunday-school Teachers' Institutes" throughout Illinois in the early 1860s. He launched a Chicago-based
magazine in 1865 and proposed for the first time a uniform lesson
plan that could be followed by teachers in all evangelical
denominations. The scheme, entitled *Two Years with Jesus: A
New System of Sunday School Study,* featured all sorts of innovations such as helpful hints for teachers and a weekly "Golden
Text" memory selection for pupils. Vincent's idea was a smash
hit in Chicago and soon he was called to New York to help the
national Methodist Church move in the same direction. His
successor as editor of the Chicago *Sunday School Teacher* was
Edward Eggleston who quickly developed a series of uniform
lessons that attracted a national following.

The Sunday school world was abuzz over Vincent's and Eggleston's work, yet it took Jacobs to make the uniform lesson plan
something, in his own inimitable phrase, "for the Sunday-schools
of this country not only; but, blessed be God! we hope, for the
world!"[7] He pushed it hard at the 1869 convention, but the target
date was 1872 when he hoped delegates would adopt this scheme:
A Lesson Committee, appointed by the big convention, would
draw up a list of scriptural topics for Sunday schools for a seven-
year cycle. Each lesson would then be studied by *every person,*
from infants to the infirm, in *every Sunday school.*

A simple idea, easily understood, it was no simply or easily
sold. Support came from old-time workers in the East but some
denominational and independent publishers were fiercely opposed to such meddling. The market for materials offered a growing, often profitable business. Jacobs' plan might subvert
denominational loyalty, quell the consumers' hunger for different material and thus affect income. This argument was seldom
openly mentioned but its reality was unquestionable. Even

Vincent and Eggleston voiced opposition along the way. Evidently knowing something of the special interests brought into committees, Eggleston said that selection of lesson texts "by a committee is fatal to aggressive action."[8]

In the meantime, Jacobs and his lieutenants massed enormous public support and enlisted rank-and-file workers. Delegates felt that they were participating in *the* decision of the century when the matter came up for a vote at the 1872 convention in Indianapolis. Some doubtless thought it a decision for eternity. The official report of that meeting records an intensity of feeling that at times "reached the morally sublime." Jacobs spoke in support of the uniform lessons when the question came up on the agenda. Not a "corporal's guard" was opposed and the victory was greeted by the convention rising to sing the "long-meter doxology."

Jacobs had won; the uniform—or International—lesson system was a fact. Whether the Sunday school had also won was the subject of a controversy that raged for fifty years. No other single action in the movement ever evoked so much praise or condemnation. Supporters defended the plan as though it were a holy cause. Moody spoke of the scheme in reverent tones twenty-four years after the 1872 action. He considered the number of newspapers that printed the weekly lesson "one of the greatest miracles ever wrought in the world" and he prayed that no one "not heaven sent" would be named to the Lesson Committee.[9]

Another observer glancing back after thirty years of experience with the uniform lessons declared that 1872 marked nothing less than the "second birth" of the movement; the point at which "the purposeless, freakish wanderings in the Scripture ceased"[10] and the Sunday schools received, as did Moses, a guiding cloud above the Tabernacle. In short, the way to the promised land was paved by uniform lessons.

Later critics were equally lavish in denunciations. Resentful of "Illinois Band" reforms, the progressive "religious educators" of the early twentieth century seized the uniform plan as a symbol of everything they deplored in the Protestant legacy. Judged by the best modern educational standards, the system was found wanting in most respects. This critique, however, substantially missed the intention of the creators. Originally the plan was a protest against inefficiency; in function and consequence, it soon became a superb organizational device to promote unity and power as well as efficiency. These are results which merit deeper scrutiny.

The World as One Massive Sunday School

Uniform lessons, for a time, gave evangelical Protestantism in the English-speaking world a common language, a Protestant version of the Roman Catholic Latin Mass of pre-Second Vatican Council days. A Sunday school attender from Boise, Idaho, could go into most denominational schools in the United States or in the Anglo-American sphere of influence and almost feel at home. It was true, as a Canadian said, that "whether you enter a Presbyterian, Baptist, Congregational, or a Methodist Sunday school, the same Scripture is read and taught."[11] This sort of uniformity eased the strains of mobility for a restless, constantly moving people. The move could be across town or across the continent; the same familiar, comforting Sunday schools were available. Or if a youngster stayed in one place during childhood, he could alternate between schools and not get much out of step. In a small Kansas town, William Allen White, the future journalist and publisher of the Emporia *Gazette,* went to four Sunday schools "for purely social reasons." At each he could expect the same question, "Now, boys, who knows the Golden Text?"[12] The arrangement was liberating for a gregarious home-town body like Willie White, as well as for a child thousands of miles from home. To be sure, Sunday schools and uniform lessons were also for adults—almost entirely in some modern rural areas with few children—but the overriding incentive throughout the movement has been directed toward the young.

Jacobs' plan heralded ecumenical unity and world brotherhood in an era largely barren of such symbols. American Christians in the closing years of the nineteenth century had few ways of celebrating an essential identity with those of different races, regions, denominations and nations. Sunday school leaders of the 1870s envisioned a new future of boundless possibilities, including complete healing of the breach between North and South.

More, they could hope for promotion of "true catholicity of feeling between Christians" which would "strike at the very roots of that narrow, unscriptural, bitter, bigoted sectarianism which has its foundations for the most part in an ignorance of God's Word."[13]

Would not all Christians hear "God's voice speaking to them the same things" if they were studying the same lessons? In retrospect the answer must be, "Not necessarily." The Sunday school vision of true catholicity proved somewhat fanciful, presupposing too much evangelical consenus about the meaning of biblical Christianity. Liturgically oriented churches, such as Episcopal and Lutheran, had considerable difficulty with the plan, if they tried it at all, because the order of lessons did not fit easily into the rhythms of the church year. Evangelical denominations—Baptist, Methodist, Presbyterian—were inclined to oversell their distinctive doctrines in "lesson helps" they sent out to parish schools. Uniform lessons did not hurt denominational publishing, which merely correlated its output with that of the Sunday School Convention cycle. That practice continues even today, for at least one adult series is still the "International Lesson" with themes set by the National Council of Churches and material prepared denominationally.

In another respect, Jacobs' scheme did succeed as a reminder of a larger unity. Uniform lessons fast became the one truly international aspect of the (U.S.-Canada) International Convention. By 1900 more than three million English pupils and teachers were using the lessons; in New Zealand, Australia, Japan, Korea, China and wherever there were British or American missionaries, the same materials were distributed. Uniform lessons were translated into forty languages and dialects for India. Worldwide use reflected the expanding reach of the transatlantic Protestant empire across the globe. The sun may never have set upon the British political empire in the late Victorian era and neither did it on Protestantism's sphere of influence. Protestants might forget the evangelical empire during the week, but they could not easily overlook it on Sunday when they engaged in the International Lesson. Shailer Mathews, a twentieth-century scholar, recalls "something inspiring" in the widespread study of the same

Sunday school lesson during his Gilded Age childhood.[14] Some thought the uniform plan a patch of heaven on earth—one school, text and weekly lesson for a durable spiritual empire.

The "Jacobites" wanted to make the Sunday school visible, to put it on the map as a prominent and inescapable feature of the American landscape. One goal was to help the greatest number possible and this could be done only by tapping the secular press. The American Sunday School Union, in the early nineteenth century, was content to publish books, magazines and tracts and to hold occasional public rallies—inadequate methods in a society where newspapers and popular magazines were increasingly the arbiters of public opinion. Generalissimo Jacobs went after the widest publicity for the weekly texts and lesson notes, and the skill of the evangelical organizers in attracting newspaper interest was no small reason why the Sunday school did become visible in the final decades of the nineteenth century. Moody was not unduly exaggerating when he rhapsodized about the miracle of newspaper coverage. The lesson with "Golden Text" was often the big religious news of the week. A spirited competition developed among syndicated columnists who wrote commentaries on Bible passages chosen by Sunday school moguls. For a brief time it seemed as though the International Lesson Committee really was determining the intellectual and religious diet of North American Protestants. Of course, newspaper-reading Catholics and Jews were being exposed to the evangelical point of view. (Perhaps Catholic diocesan weeklies started in part as a reaction to the evangelical domination of religious news in the secular press in the late nineteenth century.)

Members of the Lesson Committee did not pretend to be "dictators of the human conscience," a phrase flamboyantly used by the American Union's Publication Committee. But they were conscious of a new-found prominence which, in turn, brought pressures to yield to the blandishments of special interest groups. Advocates of the missionary cause wanted their fair share of "missionary lessons." Likewise, the Women's Christian Temperance Union (WCTU) insisted on its pound of flesh.

After all, as Frances E. Willard reminded the International Convention of 1890, the ladies with the white ribbons had served the Sunday school well. "We are not an outside force, but part and parcel of yourselves," Miss Willard declared, noting that out of 466 delegates to the 1889 WCTU convention less than half a dozen remained seated when Sunday school workers were asked to stand. "We rejoice in the international Sunday-school lessons"; she continued, "they are the first great reciprocity treaty among the nations; they are God's blessed John the Baptist of universal peace." Therefore she felt free to make the pitch for payment. "We ask you . . . to give us specific temperance lessons at least four times a year." That was first in a list of requests ending with a pledge to retain no teacher "whose breath reveals familiarity with the wine cup, the beer mug or the demijohn."[15]

Miss Willard's petition was audacious but understandable. The Sunday school had developed into a legitimate target for pressure groups, an unanticipated consequence of visibility. While the evangelical organizers wanted to avoid all controversy, including that sure to result from meeting the WCTU demand, they knew the temperance movement could stir up an even bigger ruckus. But they were comforted by the indirect assurance that Sunday school had "arrived" and the WCTU got its quarterly temperance lessons.

Evangelical Protestant zeal for efficiency reached its pinnacle in Sunday schools using uniform lessons. The degree of efficiency attainable was nowhere better demonstrated than in Philadelphia. One sight to see in 1876 was the city's centennial exposition on American progress. Another was Bethany Sunday School, the largest in North America and, some thought, the best in the world. Bethany itself was a sign of progress, a school attracting, handling and teaching thousands of youngsters. Its creator and major benefactor was John Wanamaker, both a daring merchant and renowned Sunday school superintendent. Wanamaker was dissatisfied with the old religious education and the old mercantile ways. He believed Sunday schools and stores could best serve by being more efficient. For one thing, advertising should be used. His theory was to make an enterprise known, then make it attractive and serviceable. Wanamaker applied similar principles in running his innovative department store and his Sunday school; yet it is incorrect to say the latter was a carbon copy of the merchandise outlet. Sometimes the reverse was true.

The matter of dealing efficiently with throngs of people—the issue Wanamaker confronted and solved at Bethany and at his store—was crucial to the Sunday school movement. The Philadelphia merchant was actually a rarity among local superintendents and the organizers knew the much-heralded "Sunday school Army" was a corps of volunteers with unskilled and often marginal commitment. What they needed was a simple, efficient, sabotage-proof system that could be run by amateurs. Uniform lessons seemed to fill the bill. The system would be a boon to family study, thereby reducing the load on teachers; more substitute teachers would be available since everybody in a community would know the lesson, and teacher training would be simplified.

If the new lesson plan was the answer in dealing with masses, Jacobs and his crowd reasoned, the movement could get on with its fundamental work which was expansion until the life of every single person was touched. Nothing else would suffice. The organizers had a specific vision of the Heavenly City: *the world as one massive Sunday school.* This image of the future reflected a peculiar compound of evangelical passion and American "populism." For the most part, the organizers were evangelical in motivation as well as belief: their business as Christians was to "save souls"! Not all embraced Moody's pessimism about the world as a wrecked vessel, but they accepted his conception of mission as saving as many persons as possible. The accent was on the mass rather than the single individual and his development.

Sunday school leaders were also faithful to the principle, first enunciated by Lyman Beecher and reflected in the tradition, that the Sunday school belonged to everyone. The populist principle was marshaled in a quarrel with scholarly critics who found the uniform lessons simplistic. Sunday school leaders argued that if they followed the advice of the "intellectuals" their movement would be reduced to a plaything for an elite. A populist-minded speaker at the 1899 International Convention declared his heritage as a "common man" and continued:

I believe that the greatest blessings of the International Lesson System has been that it has been . . . for the use and edification of the common people. A man said to me not long ago, "O, it is not scholarly; you want something scholarly." Well, the average man or woman, boy or girl, is not a bookworm, is not permitted to have a library in his room, to devote himself to theological studies, to scholarly Bible work.

The "Illinois Band" and friends never accepted the verdict of critics who judged uniform lessons inefficient and ineffective as a curriculum base. The scheme was, in short, the monument of a generation, so expressive of a perspective on life that it became the very symbol of the evangelical faith, for its organizers and for those in succeeding generations who shared the same values. Adult classes in northern Alabama and southern Montana still study a temperance lesson once a quarter.

The End of an Era

At the outset of the twentieth century the Sunday school seemed ready for another hundred years of dazzling growth. Horatio Alger had slipped into the act after all. Numbers had more than doubled in the thirty years after the International Convention of 1875. Workers included the best-known names in American business: John D. Rockefeller was superintendent of a Cleveland Sunday school, while Mrs. Rockefeller served as head of his primary department and their children were often drafted as supply teachers; H. J. Heinz, later described by *The Christian Century* as the man "who would rather be remembered as a Sunday school philanthropist than as the country's most successful 'pickle man,' "[16] and, of course, John Wanamaker who lived until 1922. When Wanamaker was appointed Postmaster General by President Harrison in 1889, he was willing to let others run the store but not to give up a weekly trip to Philadelphia to supervise activities at Bethany.

There were other heartening signs. The first World Sunday School Convention in 1889 was a triumph for Anglo-American initiative. Sunday school forces were chalking up successes in the drive for prohibition. They claimed to have closed down North Dakota and helped to undo booze in Kansas and other states. Some sniffed at Sunday school politics while others saw the movement as a formidable opponent. In either case, the Sunday school was deeply involved in controversial matters, thus setting a precedent for the Social Gospel and later social-action teachings. Controversies were inevitable if the movement was to meet the challenges, promises and demands of the future in a new century. As one worker said in 1902, "God seems to be offering to America the leadership of the world. . . . In a peculiar and special sense this International Convention seems to have been put in trust of the Gospel and of the world's destiny."[17]

The trust was awesome and so were some of the problems on the horizon, although most partisans had a confident air. Knowledgeable observers were beginning to worry about such problems as finding successors for the "Illinois Band." Jacobs died in 1902. John Vincent was a Methodist bishop, still involved in Sunday school work but also giving considerable energy to that huge cultural enterprise, Chautauqua, which he had helped found as a "National Sabbath-School University." No other leaders of comparable stature had appeared on the scene.

Equally vexing was the criticism heaped upon the uniform lessons. Derisive jokes about "the international game of hop, skip and jump" used by the committee in choosing texts were nothing new. In the 1890s the jeering about "the erratic work of careless shears and paste-pot" was more difficult to ignore. Even among the advocates of prohibition, quarterly temperance lessons were in trouble. "No Lesson Committee," wrote one friendly critic, "can find in the Bible four lessons a year, for five or seven years, that squarely teach total abstinence."[18]

Then, too, the movement had to defend itself against the unwelcome intrusion of modern biblical scholarship, that disconcerting importation of textual and scientific "higher criticism" from the European continent. Within the womblike comfort of a large convention it was reassuring to hear that "Germany would not be in the grip of anti-Biblical criticism today had her children enjoyed equal privileges with ours in the curriculum of the Sabbath school."[19] Or to know that the Sunday school below the Mason-Dixon line was safe because "the religious life of the South has not yielded to some influences, which elsewhere, for a while at least, boded no good to the cause of Christianity. . . . We believe that the old Book can take care of itself."[20]

The Bible emerged as "the old Book," *the* bulwark against error, something out of the past to be resolutely defended against the evolutionists and theological heretics. While admitting room for biblical scholarship elsewhere, the Lesson Committee reported in 1893 that "we can not have scientific study in the Sunday school. It would require a search with lighted candles to find either higher or lower critics in our ordinary Sunday-school classes." The need, the argument went, was to make the Bible *plain* to the common people instead of introducing into lessons "the melancholy jargon" of critics.

A similar defensive spirit pervaded the response to the American metropolis and its religious needs. Almost all populists have some exception in mind in their praise of the "people" and Sunday school leaders did not break the pattern. Like Theodore Frelinghuysen in the 1850s, they were appalled by the new immigrants washing up on the New World shore. "Now it is well known to our American delegates," said one U. S. speaker at the 1889 World Sunday School Convention in London, "that the city of New York is not an American city. . . . We would be glad if a great many more [immigrants] came from England than from other parts, because we have a great many with us whom we cannot call brethren." The "un-American" cities gave the Sunday school its most severe challenge as the century ended. An Iowan, raising the question of the frontier's location, said Sunday school discussions in his area were turning to the missionary grounds of the East and to the pressing issue, "How shall we evangelize Chicago? How shall we aid her in the suppression of anarchy? Or rather, in the suspension of anarchy at the end of a rope?"[21]

The frontier had shifted to the cities. A veteran worker in New York was sure the "Anarchist" had three Sunday schools of his own in Chicago and would soon have some in Manhattan, teaching men to hate God and their fellows. The changing city seemed hostile and could not be accepted as a natural habitat by most Sunday school workers, who in a paradoxical way must have felt much like the newcomers disembarking on Ellis Island, lonely aliens on foreign soil.

Late nineteenth-century Sunday school leadership was no less awkward in efforts to help black Sunday schools. They tried any number of black-oriented experiments in the 1890s and 1900s. The International Convention hired black staff members to develop parallel organizational structures, that is, conventions at state and local levels, among the "colored people." Later, foundations and white workers sponsored special programs in black teacher training across the South. These tactics were largely unsatisfactory. The top echelon in the movement could never shake a feeling of guilt about their continuing failure to aid black Sunday schools. That failure reflected the vast chasm between black and white America.

The B. F. Jacobs forces were unable to discern or appreciate the unique contribution of the black Sunday school in those crucial years after the Civil War. In the South, for example, Sunday classes for blacks often had to take over the task of teaching reading and writing. As one black Sunday school veteran tried to tell the International Convention in 1881, Sunday instruction served as the "common school" of his people. Carter Woodson, one of the first historians of Negro education in America, had a similar impression about the important role black Sunday schools filled in bringing literacy to the recently freed slaves.

While all who have studied the subject lack extensive firsthand sources, it was Woodson's speculation that many blacks were able after emancipation to do openly what had been only covertly possible before: learn to read and write on Sunday—first learning the alphabet, then small words, and finally reading the Bible. The compelling motive, Woodson said, was for a "better knowledge of one's Christian duty and the reward awaiting the faithful. *Many of these Negroes often learned more on a single Sunday than the average student acquired in a day school during aa week.*" [22]

Black colleges in the South, once they were started after the Civil War, seem to have sometimes included Sunday schools in which the faculty would teach. The colleges frequently had black congregations as bases and teachers understood when hired that they had responsibility in both college and Sunday school. The latter was designed to reach youths who could not qualify for the higher academic program. Both Woodson's theory and the links between black colleges and Sunday teaching indicated that the black Sunday school had its own distinctive work to do in the late nineteenth century. The elaborate paraphernalia of the white Sunday school convention was mostly irrelevant—a fact which the evangelical organizers did not clearly understand.

A leadership vacuum, the challenges of the city and the black Sunday schools—these were the big problems. But most irritating of all was the growing ridicule of the Sunday school. It was trivial but deflating. Earlier in the nineteenth century the critics had been apprehensive about the movement's strength and vitality; by the 1890s, however, fewer of them were willing to take it seriously. A crop of disdainful phrases appeared in everyday speech: innocent as a Sunday school picnic, naïve as Sunday school faith, sincere as a Sunday school voice. Mark Twain had fun with the last phrase in his account of how Tom Sawyer beat the system of memorizing Bible verses. Mr. Walters, Tom's Sunday school superintendent, "was very earnest of mien, and very sincere and honest at heart; and he held sacred things and places in such reverence, and so separated them from worldly matters, that unconsciously to himself his Sunday-school voice had acquired a peculiar intonation which was wholly absent on weekdays."[23]

Some humor was light. "When is a school not a school?" Answer, "When it's a Sunday school." And then there was a savage kind. In the fall of 1900 John D. Rockefeller, Jr., became leader of the Men's Bible Class of the Fifth Avenue Baptist Church in New York City, succeeding Charles Evans Hughes, later Chief Justice of the U. S. Supreme Court. The new teacher soon attracted all manner of attention from the newspapers, partly because the name Rockefeller symbolized everything that outraged them about American business and partly because the Sunday school was ripe for jest. "With his hereditary grip on a nation's pocketbook," said the *Pittsburgh Press*, "his talks on spiritual matters are a tax on piety." Cartoonists had a field day. The New York *Journal* depicted Rockefeller in front of his class holding a Bible, tickertape spewing from his mouth.[24] The caption read, "The Modern Sunday School." Sunday schools had become highly visible, perhaps more visible and vulnerable than the "Illinois Band" had bargained for.

Even so, a "last hurrah" for the era of Jacobs and his group was heard in Washington, D. C. in 1910 at the World's Sixth Sunday School Convention. None other than President William Howard

Taft addressed the global conclave, assuring delegates that, "No matter what views are taken or general education, we all agree —Protestant, Catholic and Jew alike—that Sunday-school education is absolutely necessary to secure moral uplift and religious spirit." Taft's words, which may have offended Catholics and Jews, were an unwitting portent of pluralism and the vagueness of American religion in the twentieth century.

But in 1910 a glorious past could be enjoyed in momentary relaxation about the future. Congress adjourned so members could walk in the grand parade, a festive occasion despite a heavy downpour of rain. Spectators along the route glimpsed such banners as "The Saloon Must Go," "Justice [David Josiah] Brewer was a Sunday School Teacher," "The Men of America for the Man of Galilee," and "Taft is Square on the Sunday School." A rousing booster spirit abounded in special yells from the various delegations as they passed the reviewing stand:

> Colorado is big, Colorado is great,
> We are the only centennial state;
> We have gold in our mines; we have silver galore,
> We have money in banks and goods in our stores;
> But the brightest assets in our glorious state
> Are the workers for God that our Sunday schools make.

The most touching gesture of all was the song of the Illinois delegation:

> Not without thy wondrous glory, / Illinois, Illinois,
> Can be writ the nation's glory, / Illinois, Illinois,
> On the record of thy years / Dwight L. Moody's name appears,
> Jacobs, Reynolds and our tears, / Illinois, Illinois.

It was a poignant appeal to the glories of the past. Moody and Reynolds—these two comrades who had made a pact in 1864 to capture a state Sunday school convention—had answered their last roll call; so had Generalissimo Jacobs. Even though world and North American Sunday school conventions would continue for many decades, in 1910 a dream was fading. It was the end of an era.

CHAPTER V

Old-Time School vs.
New-Time School

*We might as well admit it: the Sunday school is
dead.* [1]

— a church professional

*The Sunday school is the "most indispensable
institution in America."* [2]

— an "old-timer"

A few conscientious observers at the world Sunday school parade
in 1910 would happily have sung "Shall We Gather at the River?"
one last time and laid the "Army of the Lord" to rest in Arlington
National Cemetery. Announcements of the imminent or late demise of the Sunday school movement began when the twentieth
century was budding and have continued with regularity since.
In truth, the Washington gathering was one of the movement's
last superspectaculars; chief executives since President Taft
have not often extolled it as necessary for national moral uplift
nor has Congress adjourned for Sunday school parading. But neither has the institution vanished, despite the fact that the twentieth-century Sunday school epic has contained no particularly
noteworthy personalities, no heroics. Compared to the nine-

.eenth century, the story is bland. Yet there is drama, the drama of how an institution judged passé by the "better" critics and professional theorists refused to die.

Criticism of all schools is a recurring American pastime, but none has been so savagely attacked since 1900 as the Sunday school. Assaults upon public schools usually arouse a vigorous defense from well-known, influential persons. The admirers of the Sunday School, however, have gone largely unheard in the midst of the chorus of detractors. One of the foremost Protestant educators of the 1920s doubted that Sunday instruction could ever recover a genuine educational purpose since, he said, the traditions, the unpaid teaching force, the lack of standards, the curriculum and the clergy were all "against it."[3]

The outmoded Sunday school, so its critics have proposed, should be replaced by weekday ecumenical programs, study *about* religion in public schools, released-time programs, family-centered instruction, or vacation church schools. Name changes have seemed advisable on numerous occasions. Early in the century the label "church school" was put forth to avoid the "repellent" overtones of the past. That name was adopted by some denominations; the Methodists in local churches of the 1940s had virtual pitched battles between "church school" and "Sunday school" devotees, with the former winning in official policy. Others have preferred to call it "the Sunday morning session of the school of the Church."

When the ailing patient did not die before mid-century, John Wanamaker's pet institution became the object of that hostility that human beings reserve for the dying. In the 1940s it was variously described as a "menace," or an "hour of charm."[4] Charles Clayton Morrison, the renowned editor of *The Christian Century,* found the Sunday school a convenient scapegoat for all sorts of skulduggery. He accused the single weekly hour led by volunteer teachers of causing a downward curve in religious literacy and respect for religion. Shaking his finger at the Sunday school, Morrison moaned that "American society has become a secular-minded society."[5]

If there is cognizance of such things on the bank of the "river that flows by the throne of God," a company of the saints who wrote Sunday school obituaries are probably embarrassed, for it has outlived them, and in a relatively unreformed state has outlived a host of reformers. The folkways of popular religion are never easily altered, but the grip of habit and custom only partly explains why the old-time Sunday school has persisted despite its death notices. As inherited, the cause has remained a lively one for millions of Christians who have refused in the twentieth century to abandon a treasured institution without a struggle.

The ensuing fight became symbolic of a deep split within American Protestantism. On one side were the church *professionals,* a new breed ready and determined to reform Sunday school in accordance with changing dictates of modern culture. From the early years of the twentieth century to the 1940s the professional banner was carried by the "religious educators." The next generation—the postliberal church educators and their successors—continued the professionals' fight after World War II. On the other side was a shifting array of opposing forces. Most obvious were the *old-timers,* the evangelicals who wanted to keep the Sunday school much as it was in the days of B. F. Jacobs. In addition, many laymen maintained a quiet but steady underground resistance against the reformers. The lengthy conflict shaped up more like the entrenched snarling along the Hindenburg line in World War I than the decisive Allied route at El Alamein in World War II. Timetables have varied from place to place and sniper fire is still heard today. Of course, inertia has figured in the story as a force often playing into the hands of old-timers. These modern tensions over the Sunday school reveal much more about the multi-layered nature of Protestant culture than do historical approaches sampling only the currents in theologies, denominational polities and ecumenical strata.

"Middletown," 1910-1945: The Disappointment of the Professionals

Henry Seidel Canby, once editor of *The Saturday Review of Literature,* remembered Sunday school in the 1890s as a time of "Bible stories parroted by misses doing their duty, and of a catechism as meaningless in that untheological age as a treatise on alchemy, yet memorized and rememorized." Many youngsters had similar experiences, because Sunday school was not a school in any acceptable meaning of the word so much as an integral part of a unique and forgotten set of activities forming the Victorian Sabbath. The fabric of that day had many strands: church, Sunday school, special clothes; roast beef and the Sunday newspaper for more casual families; and cold meat, hymn sings, Bible reading and peaceful walks for stricter households. The day was extraordinary. "For with clean collar and cuffs and a Sunday suit, one put on decorum," Canby recalled, "and in the calm of the quiet neighborhood the mind relaxed, and when the bells began, the slow march of so many church-goers ranged by families, and dressed for a rite, stirred in the consciousness a sense of immemorial . . . custom."[6]

Sharing the same memory but not relishing it were the religious educators, a new generation in a different world from that of B. F. Jacobs. They were college-trained, attracted to the progressive spirit of John Dewey in education and the Social Gospel of Walter Rauschenbusch in theology, and unafraid of the latest scholarly judgment of biblical critics. This able, up-to-date crowd wanted, above all, a religion appealing to like-minded moderns. Obviously, the old Sunday school would no longer do; whatever the other disagreements of the religious educators, they agreed on that point. The new breed respected the dedicated volunteers, the "misses doing their duty," but entertained no nostalgia about Sunday school as part and parcel of immemorial custom. After all, the progressives reasoned, the institution was barely over a hundred years old and already stale and irrelevant; it represented the wrong kind of permanence in a rapidly changing society. The Sunday school had to be reformed.

In passing, it should be said that the reformers frequently turned to Horace Bushnell, the nineteenth-century liberal, for support, and they appropriated that intellectual giant in a historically peculiar way. Bushnell contributed little to the Sunday school movement in his day, 1802-1876, for his contention that children should be raised as if they had always been Christian flew in the face of Sunday school ideology in the mid-nineteenth century when youngsters were treated as "little adults needing conversion." By appealing to Bushnell within a Sunday school context, religious educators gave their reforming ideas an undeserved appearance of maturity. They also created the impression, which too few historians have bothered to correct, that Bushnellian "Christian nurture" was an integral part of popular Protestant education.

Uniform lessons were a special symbol of the old-fashioned way. The plan violated the religious educators' common sense and their psychological views; it was educational absurdity to subject persons of different ages to the same lesson. What a child understands and *needs*—a new word soon turned into a cliché in the lexicon of Protestant education—was not always fitting for adults, they claimed. Even more, what makes sense to adults is often mystifying and bewildering to small children. Such criticism of the uniform lessons was not without substance: in the fall of 1906 a four-year-old boy started his Christian schooling with a lesson on the problem of whose wife a woman would be in the resurrection when she had married seven men. Furthermore, the Bible was badly mangled. Old Testament lesson favorites, picked because they presumably interested youngsters, were Joseph, David, and Daniel in the lions' den, while prophets got short shrift except for occasional temperance sessions plucked out of Amos. Willard Uphaus, the peace radical and a religious educator in the 1920s, put his finger on a real weakness of uniform lessons. He noted that the hopping and skipping from one part of the Bible to another gave children little chance to "comprehend the long-time historical development . . . of the ethical and religious concepts being taught them. . . ."[7]

Further, religious educators charged that traditional curriculum neglected the interests and affections of adolescents. Here was a fairly new concern. The notion of adolescense as a separate stage of life did not emerge until the latter part of the nineteenth century. Teenagers gained the spotlight only after education for industrial society gradually lengthened the time spent in school and, consequently, postponed full adult responsibility. Protestants in the 1880s and 1890s introduced questions still in vogue today: Can the church "hold on" to teenagers? Can sexual potency be contained during that increasingly long stretch between puberty and marriage? Both questions bothered the imaginations of Sunday educators.

Organizations to meet the *needs* of adolescents came into the picture. One model was Christian Endeavor, founded in 1881 by a Congregational minister in Portland, Maine, but the denominations were not willing to let too much money or energy be squandered on interdenominational outfits. The Methodist Epworth League and the Baptist Young People's Union of America were started by 1889. Well into the twentieth century, countless new adult-inspired efforts to capture the attention of youth were set in motion, using passwords, secret formulas, uniforms, membership badges, and rafts of officers. The ancient ideal of knighthood inspired several groups. Knights of the Holy Grail had as its motto, "Confession, Chastity, Charity."

None of this quite stilled the anxiety and edginess of church fathers about the challenges presented by teenagers. Sunday school publications in the twentieth century's first quarter were filled with warnings against "poolroom habits," admonitions to boys not to think about sex, and attacks on the "degrading" teachings of the street. The 1911 International Sunday School Convention introduced a Department of Purity to instill the ideals of the "white life," a Victorian euphemism for sexual abstinence. Religious educators were sympathetic to these initiatives but knew the Sunday school had a long way to go in dealing adequately with adolescents.

Basically, the reformers were embarrassed by Sunday school ineptitude as an educational venture. Public schools overshadowed the church programs, whose progressive edges were few and whose most visible symbols of backwardness were its facilities. Quarters were often nothing more than the church basement, those "cold, gloomy underground rooms delicately frescoed with furnace pipes."[8] Or if a nineteenth-century congregation could afford an educational "plant," it was usually modeled on the Akron plan—a cavernous theater with the superintendent's desk on the stage and partitioned alcoves for classes around the edge of the auditorium. The Akron design, first used in that Ohio city, was considered the best form for any school featuring uniform lessons: the superintendent could conduct the opening exercises, keep an eye on classes and then review the lesson at the close, all from the lofty splendor of his desk. By 1910 most "new" Sunday school buildings had encased the outmoded uniform lesson plan in expensive brick and mortar. The remains of that enthusiasm dot the land today, but the stages have come in handy for congregations trying to "hold on" to teenagers through drama ministries.

Mortifying to the religious educators was the gimmick-ridden appeal of the average Sunday program. The old-timers had resorted to a variety of promotional techniques to sustain and increase their booming enterprise. A loyal Sunday school army was a popular way of maintaining attendance and discipline: "On Time Every Time, A Learned Lesson Every Time, and An Offering for Christ Every Time." An "On Timer's Tribe" had a "pledge to bind and a pin to remind." Local schools had rally days, decision days, children's days, concerts and picnics. National organizations abounded for each age group with headquarters, mottos and special songs.

The religious educators looked upon this hustle and bustle as empty efforts of well-intentioned workers, amateurs who had too long dominated the Sunday school. Amateurism was, in fact, the nub of their quarrel with the traditional movement. *Professional* leadership must take over. And why not? Experts were evident in public schools, social work and municipal life. Should Protestant education be different? Volunteer leaders, in the reformers' scheme, should be aided by a full-time "director of religious education" if a congregation could afford one. If not, the minister was expected to assume the mantle of the professional. At the very least a specialist should be at work in every state and denominational center. The formula was straightforward: no professional, no reform; no reform, no school worthy of respect.

Few groups were more insistent upon that formula than the independent Religious Education Association formed in 1903 at the instigation of President William Rainey Harper of the University of Chicago. A man of many talents, Harper had a long-standing interest in popularizing the scholarly study of scripture. His pioneering work on biblical correspondence courses was, in part, a flank attack upon the uniform lessons. So, too, was the creation of the Association. Its founders included some of the most illustrious names in university and religious life at the turn of the century. This small agency developed into a "brain trust" for the reformers who hoped to transform the Sunday school into a thoroughly modern institution.

If the Association was the "brain trust," the International Council of Religious Education was the organizing center of the updating movement. The Council, founded in 1922, was a single expression of both the Sunday school convention heritage and the concerns of powerful denominational boards of education. It represented the aspiring professional's best chance for a major breakthrough. Within the Council a staff of well-trained educators laid out ambitious plans for sweeping changes in the curricular diet of Sunday schools. Their proposed "International curriculum" was far more than just a replacement for the old-style uniform lesson plan; it was to embody the latest findings in education. The era of "graded lessons" had finally arrived, after long years of preparation.

Graded lessons depended on the insights and theories of such men as John Dewey, William James and E. L. Thorndike whose approaches became pervasive in public education during the early twentieth century. Foremost was the necessity to take account of motivation, stages of maturity and gradations of learning ability. Small, successive steps were deemed more appropriate in the learning process than full and repeated exposure to a whole corpus of information. Taking seriously the developmental needs of each age group, religious educators prepared Sunday school materials and teaching guides for infants, toddlers, primary elementary pupils, older elementary children, junior high school youngsters, senior highs, older youths, young married adults, mature adults and senior adults. Pleasant physical surroundings conducive to learning at each particular age were recommended. Cribs, three or four sizes of ribbed-back Sunday school chairs for children, and classroom decorative material appeared in supply catalogs.

To their credit, religious educators imbued with Deweyian psychology pushed beyond the Akron plan in church school facilities. They were often successful in persuading congregations that learning was enhanced by settings more comfortable and functional than auditoriums with partitioned cubbyholes. The reformers were most adventurous in organizing a farflung program in teacher training. At least for a while the Sunday school teachers seemed almost abreast of public school counterparts in exposure to the latest and best educational thinking.

For all their new-found expertise, the religious educators were never able to generate the kind of mass enthusiasm which prevailed in the golden days of the nineteenth century. At that time the visible leaders of the movement had been laymen such as B. F. Jacobs and John Wanamaker. By 1930, however, the old-style volunteers had been eased out of seats on top-level boards supposedly directing Sunday school affairs. The full-time professional was clearly in charge and the volunteers were treated, perhaps unconsciously, as potential trainees, the beneficiaries of the experts' guidance. Local teachers—laymen—resented the apparent condescension from on high.

Then, too, the religious educators' version of progressivism was abstract and vaguely unsettling to the mass of workers. In the old days the purpose of teaching was reasonably clear: conversion. For instance, when the senior Rockefellers settled in New York and took up Sunday school labors along the Hudson, Mrs. Rockefeller kept track of her pupils by listing their names in a notebook, with a capital C before those who were orthodox Christians. After one name she added this note, "Died July 2, 1894, the first to go and not a Christian."[9] Mrs. Rockefeller's evangelical certainty was not shared by twentieth-century religious educators who tended to indulge in blurry talk of "righteous living" and Christian "character education"—goals difficult to translate into classroom practicalities for teachers who spent only two or three hours per week on Sunday school matters. Similarly, the methods of progressive education—the experience-centered approach with a stress on problem-solving and attention to student needs—required a sophistication and commitment of time unavailable among rank-and-file volunteers.

Not surprisingly, religious educators were poorly received in the hinterlands, and also rather coolly welcomed by fellow professionals in the public sector. Was all the fuss about religious education necessary when public schools were doing so well in the formation of character? "In its earlier stages," Shailer Mathews bitingly commented, "religious education was secular education dressed in a Prince Albert coat."[10]

Meanwhile, the life of the ordinary Sunday school went on much as it had, routines and customs changing little. B. F. Jacobs would have felt right at home in most classes in the 1920s, especially in "Middletown," that typical American community made famous by Robert and Helen Lynd in their epoch-making sociological study. The Lynds reported some variations between schools and modest improvements here and there, but for the most part, they said, "going to Sunday School is much the same sort of activity in all classes and in all churches and has changed relatively little since the nineties." The Lynds' description of an average Sunday school included everything the religious educators disliked:

A noisy earnestness characterizes the opening exercises, punctuated with much bustling to and fro by late-comers and secretaries. Hymns are sung lustily, especially the favorites with repeated choruses such as "I'm going to go to glory by and by." During the prayers of the superintendent adults may utter frequent "Amens," while restless children stare about or idly pinch each other. The whole school listens to the reading of the lesson, after which it breaks up into little groups scattered through the room, each with an earnest teacher leaning over the back of the pew in front, facing his class. . . . [about thirty minutes later classes are] interrupted by a bell from the platform, and the superintendent asked for "anybody wishing to leave a message"; there being no answer, the collection was announced, school papers distributed, and the school clattered out into the sunshine.[11]

Judged by religious educators' standards, the Sunday school in "Middletown" was a disaster. While hundreds of similar communities filled the countryside, the reformers could point to few models embodying their ideology.

"Give Me That Old-Time" School: 1910-1945

Soon after the Wall Street crash of 1929, the professionals could have begun preparing for defeat at the grass roots. First, the depression erased many traces of their reformist activity, mainly because they lost the battle of the budget. Professional workers cost money, but the old-style Sunday school was inexpensive as well as durable. Then came the blow of a new theology seeping in from Europe in the 1930s and 1940s. Religious educators had hooked their cause to liberal theology, in America a blend of historical progressivism and the Social Gospel. The new theology, stemming from such figures as Karl Barth and Reinhold Niebuhr, enjoyed a period of popularity during which liberalism was discredited.

Next, the reformers' image of the future proved too optimistic. They anticipated a future of slow but unending progress just as they believed in the possibility of continual growth for each individual—a persuasion typical of that idealistic generation whose formative years came around the turn of the century. Many Americans of that time, as one interpreter has put it, saw "the main guarantee of universal morality . . . neither in the mind of God nor in argument nor in tradition, but in the *unfolding American future.*" [12] Actually, the goal they held was not vastly different from Lyman Beecher's desire to reconcile national prosperity with purity and future blessedness. Hope in America's future provided the courage to take on the complex task of remaking a well-established institution, carving out a new profession and reforming popular religious opinions. It was admittedly an audacious task for a small band of seminary professors, church bureaucrats and their followers. If the original Sunday school backers, relatively few, could attract an aroused constituency, why not the religious educators? They thought they could gather troops, and expected a mass movement based on American common sense. Even more important, they presupposed that people are pragmatic, mentally alert and steeped in democratic love. Children are innately curious, intelligent, healthy-minded persons who would someday help remake the world. Therein, they thought, lay the hope of the future.

Sadly for the hopeful, twentieth-century America experienced a different kind of progress, full of ironic twists and unexpected consequences. Totally unexpected by the religious educators was the final and major reason for their decline: they simply failed to attract the needed recruits, and they alienated nonprofessional evangelicals who elected to remain outsiders to the world of scholarship, relevance and social action. Although the reformers believed firmly in democracy, they impressed opponents as another elite group trying to force their will upon the people. Staunchly against any form of clerical domination or authoritarianism in religion, they were nonetheless accused of being a new "priestly class," professionals who thought they knew what was best for others. The outreach was to all people, particularly the working class and neglected urban children. But that also failed; their gospel proved more acceptable to the middle class, people much like the reform leaders themselves.

Almost from the start of the twentieth century the hard-working amateurs of the traditional Sunday school suspected that the university-trained experts were trying to take the "college of the common people" away from those it was meant to serve. Pride mingled with earnest conviction in the old-timer who lashed out at "pretentious gentlemen" rushing into print and onto platforms to find fault with "the plain yeomanry who come from factory and office and farm, and take boys and girls an hour a week, with no other compulsion than that of love, and with little other preparation than the love of God's Book and the hope to make it an instrument of salvation to those whom they teach. . . . We have done, and are doing, a great work. The education we give is that of the heart, not the head."[13]

"Heart" and "head" once again became rival symbols. Yet whereas in church education of the nineteenth century the mind had been relegated to second place in the scale of values, the twentieth-century distinction sent the two in opposite directions within the Sunday school itself. The polarizing of heart and head was an old-timer's way of using populism against specialists. But it also meant the old-timers were turning their backs on certain intellectual and social trends at work in the culture. They relinquished their claim to an impact on the whole of American life. This, at least, was a consequence which the evangelicals seemingly had to accept to save their Sunday schools.

The crucial decade for the old-timers was the 1920s. American culture was going modern; a new mentality was celebrated in advertising, in national magazines, and on the radio. Growing, sophisticated urban styles left little room for the "better values" of old America. Small-town and rural Protestants were prepared to fight a battery of enemies—intellectual secularists, religious modernists, Catholics and minorities. The Ku Klux Klan, Prohibitionism, opposition to evolution, and the underground campaign against the Presidential candidacy of Al Smith, a Catholic, were part of that struggle. A lasting victory was scored in the restriction of immigration and a momentary one in Prohibition; but the old forces were losing on the broad scene and ultimately lost the war for censorship and against more casual manners and morals.[14]

No less threatening to the old-timers was what they saw happening in the Sunday school organizations. It was bad enough that the churches of their forefathers had warmed to liberalism. Worse yet was the way newcomers were capturing the crucial Sunday school spots. In the first thirty years of the century, denominational boards of education quietly shifted toward new operational styles, carried out by staff specialists. While few of the new men were outright biblical modernists, they talked and acted like professionals, as did the staff of the International Council of Religious Education. More was at stake than theological differences. Social and political heritages were also on the line. Fearing the end of the movement, old-timers cried out in pain; they mourned a past free of those they saw as bland experts dealing slights and snubs to the untutored. An unprecedented sort of class warfare emerged, an exercise in status politics which has become a mark of twentieth-century America. As much as financial empowerment and political success, it is *standing* which has motivated groups and individuals in the nation's brand of pluralism.

The evangelical Sunday school stalwarts did more than cry. They chose their ground, named the important work to do and refused to budge. They gave others the right to worry about the claims of the mind and, convinced that biblical scholars changed their views from day to day, turned indifferent ears to the latest opinion from the academic groves. Old-fashioned Sunday schools had no need of professors, proud scientists and new professionals who believed in the permanence of modern, liberal culture. The old-timers were not sure of the staying power of the world cherished by religious educators. The times were uncertain, and there were signs of God's coming judgment upon apostate churches and a sin-sick civilization. With a bleak future, why fret about relevance and being up to date? Two verities remained constant: the Bible as Word of God and the Sunday lesson to teach that unchanging Word. As the nation moved into World War II, the old-timers' Sunday school was still seeking conversions.

Orthodoxy Meets Neo-Orthodoxy (1945–)

On the eve of the war, the Sunday schools in mainline denominations, which for the most part had plugged into the professional education circuit, were clearly in trouble. Enrollments had been slipping for years. Between 1926 and 1936 the Methodists reported a drop of 34 per cent; Disciples of Christ fell 23 per cent and Presbyterians, U. S. A. (Northern) 18 per cent. In contrast, sects and conservative groups were growing. The Assembly of God Sunday school increased its rolls by more than 300 per cent in the same decade, and the Pentecostal Holiness schools doubled their membership.

At this low ebb for the professionals, a transfusion was in the offing: a new group of postliberal educators appeared shortly after the war to fill the role played earlier by the religious education movement. The fervor created in denominational boards of Christian education and in the National Council of Churches (one of whose founding partners in 1950 was the International Council of Religious Education) again overshadowed the plodding and productive constancy of old-time evangelicals. In fact, post-World War II America was in the grips of such a massive religious revival that streams of enthusiasm were difficult to sort out.

The changing of the professional guard was heralded by the appearance in 1948 of the neo-orthodox "Faith and Life" series of the Presbyterian Church, U.S.A. The "new curriculum," as it was known throughout the 1950s, was a stunning success, both as a fresh breeze in the musty recesses of the Sunday school world and as a profitable publishing venture. Other denominations soon followed with revamped educational programs. The 1950s was the great decade for curricular innovation and renovation. Denominational boards and their printing facilities were hives of activity. And there was, in those years of the Eisenhower Administration, a momentary upswing of interest in mainline denominational Sunday schools.

Neo-orthodoxy was the major catalyst which helped to give the professionals new vigor. This theology in America reflected Calvinism as revitalized in Europe by Emil Brunner and Karl Barth, reinforced by Reinhold Niebuhr's assertion of the doctrine of original sin. It refuted the liberal reliance on progress, electing instead to emphasize God's sovereignty and the decisive revelation of the Bible. With liberal religious education already going stale in America, the new theology was an attractive option for enlivening Sunday schools.

Not all the programs in the 1950s were as unabashedly neo-orthodox as the Presbyterian's "Faith and Life" literature. Yet each did reflect, sooner or later, the new debate stimulated by theologians in the academic market place, and all were alike in at least two respects. First, they accepted the latest findings of biblical scholars, though that may not have been unmistakably clear to their audiences. Second, the curriculum revision was, by and large, the work of professionals who wanted to combine the best of theology and modern education.

Neo-orthodoxy had evangelical qualities but it was not identical with evangelical *orthodoxy*. It was much more attuned to the winds of modernity. As much as the postliberal educators might disagree theologically with their liberal predecessors, they still retained the professional stance—an eagerness to popularize current thought emanating from seminary and university, serious respect for the discoveries of professionals in the field of psychology, a drive for relevance, a zeal for public issues and an imperative to engage in social action. Catching up with Sunday school trends, *Time* magazine reported in late 1962 that "no longer does a teacher go into class armed only with the Good Book and a supply of patience built up over the previous six days. He is likely to have a skeleton text, a book of suggested activities, a visual-aid kit, and the advice of a child psychologist."[15]

As might have been expected, the postliberals found themselves in the same sort of trouble with their constituencies as did the religious educators. The new material was sometimes difficult to understand and hard for teachers to use despite a surge of training sessions. Besides, it mixed religion and politics. "Why can't we have something like they used in the good old days?" became a common plaintive plea.

The postliberals were no more successful than the liberals in scotching what seemed to sophisticated minds to be bizarre methods of enhancing Sunday school enrollment. For example, in the fall of 1952, cowboy actor Roy Rogers and his horse Trigger put in an appearance at the Trinity Methodist Church of Los Angeles. Rogers noted that it was Trigger's first time to go to Sunday school. The San Gabriel (California) Union Church released helium-filled ballons with tracts attached to lure residents to Sunday instruction. One stunt-conscious superintendent turned himself into a modern Simeon Stylites, staying up in a eucalyptus tree for twenty hours to evoke pledges of Sunday school attendance from sympathetic witnesses.

In the 1960s the merry-go-round of theological change was moving faster. The vogue of undiluted neo-orthodoxy was waning. Publication of Harvey Cox's *The Secular City* signaled a new interest in "worldly" theology. No sooner had this perspective been incorporated into the curriculum of the mainline denominations than the needle of fashion swung unsteadily toward "death of God," "hope," "black theology" and "joy and celebration." Sunday school literature planners and writers entered the 1970s as weary victims of a one-year cultural lag. Hoping to be current, the best they could do, given publication schedules, was to keep up with what was the rage the year before.

The latter part of the 1960s also witnessed a backlash in the churches. There was a delayed reaction against civil rights militancy. The religious antiwar movement, student protests, and the new visibility of sex in public media were felt in Sunday schools. After years of relative affluence, denominational boards were now in deep financial trouble. Enrollments were declining from the 1950s' highs as the happy memory of the post-World War II religious boom faded. Protestant theology was in disarray and there was no way for church educators to keep up on all the intellectual and social action fronts or to deal with the enormous quantity of educational proposals. The eighth decade of the twentieth century opened with renewed pronouncements that the Sunday school, along with the church, and maybe God, was dead.

Yet throughout the neo-orthodox period and the kaleidoscopic theological season following, the new generation upholding the nineteenth-century evangelical spirit remained quietly optimistic about their prospects for maintaining the old forms of Sunday school. The latest recruits for the old-timers' cause still looked to the institution as a crucial bulwark for evangelical faith. That same 1962 *Time* article which observed the Sunday school teacher's dependency on the child psychologist also said: "Noting that 85 per cent of the baptisms in his denomination come by way of Sunday school, one Southern Baptist concludes that 'the greatest technique of evangelism in the twentieth century is not revivalism but the Sunday school.' "[16]

The old-timers could take comfort in the rapid growth of Sunday schools outside the mainline churches. While specialists plied their magic among static standard brand denominations, the less ecumenical churches, Pentecostals and other "fringe" groups were on the move. The handwriting on the wall was coming clear by the early 1960s. Denominations inside the National Council could not match the Sunday school growth of churches beyond the reach of typical ecumenism. The most rapidly expanding churches in the late 1960s were independent and almost fundamentalist groups, replete with Sunday schools. The old American Sunday School Union was still alive to serve the conservative Protestant sector, but a greater volume of curriculum business was done by independent companies such as David C. Cook, Gospel Light Publications and the Scripture Press. Only two of the fifty largest Sunday schools in 1970—nineteen Southern Baptist churches aside—used the literature from denominational sources. Instead, churches were buying Bible-centered, conversion-seeking materials. Most of the lessons for children were graded, a singular feature of the religious education philosophy which became standard for many evangelicals.

A majority of the largest Sunday schools were Southern Baptist, Independent Baptist, or affiliates of the Baptist Bible Fellowship. The world's largest, according to the 1970 annual tabulation of *Christian Life* magazine, was that of the Akron Baptist Temple, with a weekly attendance of 5,801. A congregation of the Baptist Bible Fellowship, this Ohio church had eight hundred volunteer staff members and an expanding fleet of buses. The guiding light of the Sunday school was Dallas Billington, founder and pastor of the Akron Temple, who set the following standards for teachers: "They can't smoke, take part in dirty stories, or go dancing. We want those who teach the Word of God to be clean."[17] Every one of the largest schools, said one investigator, was "led by an aggressive, gifted pastor, who heads up a militant program of evangelism."[18] About 75 per cent of the big schools, each with an attendance of well over a thousand, closed the Sunday programs with evangelistic appeals.

The disparity of strength between old-timers' Sunday schools and those of ecumenically inclined denominations suggested in the 1960s that leadership of the movement had already passed into the hands of custodians long ignored or rejected by the established professionals. Certainly the evangelicals were convinced the shift had taken place, that the future again belonged to them. "Spiritual emphasis characterizes the 'new look' in evangelical Sunday schools," said one of their leaders in the 1960s. "There has been a complete break with the naturalistic and coldly intellectual approach in religious education and a turn to the warmly personal and experiential appeal. . . . Evangelicals see the Sunday school as a divine institution with divine oversight, a divine mission and a divine program."[19] Many stood up to cheer "the most indispensable institution in America."

It Just Keeps Rolling Along

Final conclusions about the American Sunday school are premature because the story is unfinished. No one can yet estimate the full ramifications of the cleavage between professionals and old-timers. There are signs that the more established evangelicals are developing their own versions of a professional caste, which will doubtless inspire some future revolt of a new generation of old-timers. One example of such a struggle is appearing in the Southern Baptist Sunday school. The denomination's Sunday school board authorized a new commentary on Genesis in the late 1960s. When it appeared with full attention to scientific criticism of the scripture, the 1970 annual Southern Baptist Convention ordered it withdrawn and revised.

The expert versus volunteer struggle is substantial enough to offer a telling observation on the whole of American society: despite the rhetoric about a need for national and spiritual unity, liberal and conservative forces, specialists and common men find it nearly impossible to agree on goals and methods. The church intellectual urgently trying to reach and bring up the mass of people to his level of comprehension is often so isolated from those he seeks to touch that most of his efforts bring disappointing results. It is like a suburban civic group putting up hundreds of dollars to ask the heads of the Urban Coalition, the Urban League and the Office of Economic Opportunity to illuminate the extent of poverty, but never asking the poor from the neighboring slum to say a word.

Protestant denominations currently have, at top levels, splendidly trained staffs planning and executing thoroughly up-to-date curricula, printed with the most modern illustrations and quoting *Newsweek* right along with the Bible. But there is little chance that their constituencies will ever be much affected by this material. Nothing in tradition or in pragmatic analysis supports the likelihood that unchurched "mod" youths or the children of conservative families will be won by the literature of the major denominational boards of education.

Several other interim conclusions are possible:

1. The Sunday school continues as an enterprise of considerable magnitude and complexity, involving some 42 million persons in North America. Mainline enrollment declines and some denominations are not far from throwing in the towel, which is virtually what the United Church of Canada has done. With a decrease of over 300,000 during the 1960s, the Canadians have, by and large, decided not to perpetuate reforms aimed at enlivening

the Sunday school. Their hope is for some other type of educational device.

Today in the United States, schools are of every possible size and outlook. Observers on any Sunday morning could visit church classrooms, each embodying a different stage of the movement's development. A fair number have incorporated the spirit and sophistication of the neo-orthodox *church school* of the 1950s. Avant-grade centers exist and their experimentation represents a revival of the *progressive school* in religious education days. And the "Middletown" *Sunday school* proliferates. The largest in the early 1970s were latter-day versions of John Wanamaker's Bethany school a hundred years earlier. According to a sympathetic observer, the secret of the present success is "the energetic minister who leads his flock like a president runs a corporation."[20] With a less clerical slant, Wanamaker advocated almost the same thing.

2. Important changes have taken place over the past century. A prime example is the improvement in curricular materials from denominational and independent publishers. This has involved both choice and necessity. While Sunday school publishers generally want to keep up with the best in American education, they are also driven by what sociologist Peter Berger calls the "logic of market economics." In pluralistic societies, Berger notes, religious institutions may not take for granted the allegiance of constituencies. The tradition, once imposed by authoritative means, must be sold—"the religious institutions become marketing agencies and the religious traditions become consumer commodities."[21] Since this means more variety in materials offered, the odds are in favor of some superior literature. Whether it is properly utilized or not is another matter.

3. Despite better materials the classroom scene in most Sunday schools is approximately what it was fifty years ago. The failure of the professional church educator to dent the customs of popular Protestantism was to be expected. Typical teachers today receive about as little help and training as did their grandmothers in 1900. Most ministers remain indifferent to Sunday school

affairs unless some unusual trouble arises. A study in the mid-decades of the twentieth century indicated that pastors spent less than 5 per cent of their time on the educational work of the church, or "little more than they have to give to janitorial services."[22] Aside from the fact that it is a rare clergyman in the 1970s who wields a broom, the data is probably still reliable. Scores upon scores of Sunday schools in urban and rural areas function, as they always have, in relative separation from the rest of the church. "Sunday school is Sunday school" and "church is church" and in western Nebraska and on Tennessee's Cumberland Plateau one can skip the latter but not the former if social respectability is to be maintained. Given the tensions which have existed between Sunday school and congregation, superintendent and pastor, it is somewhat amazing that the educational program has survived at all.

All denominations are pondering ways in which Sunday schools can be maintained or reformed as vital channels of religious instruction, but black churches face special challenges introduced by the black power movement. The historic Negro communions have moved toward the preparation of educational material appropriate to the black struggle for freedom and justice. During the late 1960s, however, the liberation forces within black Christianity tended to lump the Sunday school with a kind of religion it sees as teaching subservient attitudes. Black churches, no longer needed to provide literacy, are probably harder pressed than their white counterparts to define the role of Sunday training. These denominations are basically evangelical in theology. The direction their Sunday schools take may offer an indication of how they respond to race-conscious religious militancy with a "black Christ," and not infrequently it may show open hostility to white-controlled ecumenical structures.

4. From the 1950s on, three popular attitudes toward the Sunday school have generally prevailed in the United States. The positive one was summed up by J. Edgar Hoover who, as a former superintendent, praised the Sunday school as a "crime prevention laboratory."[23] The negative assessment was put forth in a

Life magazine article that said the Sunday school is sometimes "the most wasted hour of the week."[24] The third is simple disregard. All three are off base. The crime problem is more complicated than Hoover implied; the *Life* comment is an extravagant vote of confidence in how people spend the rest of their time; and the option of disregard misses a huge segment of Americans who are just being American.

From the vantage point of the Time-Life building or the lofty professionalism of seminaries, it has been easy to overlook the Sunday school as the incarnation of popular Protestantism. It gives millions of youngsters some sense of how Protestants think, feel, act and sing. For people who have painfully discarded much of their heritage to accommodate pluralism, it is a rare "immemorial custom." In spite of all the negative evaluations of sophisticated culture, the Sunday school may add up to an educational alternative more humane than public or private institutions which have responded to industrial society's insatiable desire for more technologists and bureaucrats. Restless students have hardly asked for the tutelage of little misses doing their duty on Sunday, but they are often searching for something akin to what the Sunday school offers. They want to know what life does, or might, mean. At its best, the Sunday school has tried to illuminate Protestantism's answers to these questions. Knowing the road from Damascus to Jerusalem prior to entering the chaotic maze of modern ideologies may prepare a mind to deal with the traumas which threaten each person today. The possibility is worth contemplating.

Not so long ago in the modern technological age Willie Morris, the editor-in-chief of *Harper's* magazine, went to a Methodist Sunday school in the deep South. He recalls that

... our teacher told us stories about the Bible, or helped us make religious posters, or led us in singing: Jesus loves me! this I know. . . . Later as we grew older there would be more sophisticated Sunday School sessions, when we would sit in small circles and talk about religion and how we could get the children who had not showed up that Sunday more interested in it. We would hold hands and pray, and whisper the benediction, and dream up projects to make our class the most active in the whole church and how best to help out the preacher in his many duties. We would read Bible verses and discuss their hidden meaning.[25]

That is how it was around 1870, too. It may not be that way in the year 2000, and yet the big little school may still be around. The technological whizzes, seminary professors, liberal intellectuals and religious faddists have little idea how slowly minds change in that still forceful, white middle-class Protestant culture which largely shaped the United States. Politicians and Madison Avenue men know better and make use of the continuities. Those Protestant goals of prosperity and future blessedness—and sometimes purity—long ago became the aims of Americans of all races and religions. As long as any evangelicals remain, they will be ardently striving to put purity back in the center of the pattern for reconciliation worked out by Lyman Beecher. The chances are fairly good that the method for the task will be a Sunday school.

NOTES

Introduction

1. Jürgen Moltmann, *Theology of Hope* (New York: Harper & Row, 1967), p. 269.
2. Sam Keen, *To a Dancing God* (New York: Harper & Row, 1969), p. 9.

CHAPTER I *An Idea Whose Time Had Come*

1. Dagobert D. Runes (ed.), *The Selected Writings of Benjamin Rush* (New York: Philosophical Library, 1947), p. 88.
2. Perry Miller, *The Life of the Mind in America* (New York: Harcourt, Brace and World, Inc., 1965), p. 7.
3. Daniel Dorchester, *Christianity in the United States* (New York: Phillipps and Hunt, 1888), p. 426.
4. G. Webster, *Memoir of Robert Raikes* (Nottingham: G. W. Webster, 1873), p. 15.
5. Joseph Ivimey, *Memoir of William Fox, Esq.* (London: printed for George Wightman, 1831), p. 18.
6. Jonas Hanway, "A Comprehensive SENTIMENTAL BOOK for scholars learning in Sunday Schools," included in *A Comprehensive View of Sunday Schools* (London: N.P., 1786), pp. 12, 13.
7. William Jones, *Memoir of the Rev. Rowland Hill* (London: Henry G. Bohn, 1853), p. 413.
8. Ford K. Brown, *Fathers of the Victorians* (Cambridge at the University Press, 1961), p. 4.
9. *Ibid.,* pp. 327-28.

10. Cited by Rowland Hill, *An Apology for Sunday Schools* (London: C. Whittingham, 1801), p. vii.
11. Robert Kelley, *The Transatlantic Persuasion* (New York: Alfred A. Knopf, 1969), p. 157.
12. *Ibid.*, p. 112.
13. George W. Bethune, *Memoirs of Mrs. Joanna Bethune* (New York: Harper & Brothers, 1863), p. 120.
14. E. O. Jameson, *Historical Discourse* (Boston: Alfred Mudge and Son, 1877), p. 82.
15. James I. Brownson, *A History of the First Presbyterian Church of Washington, Pa.* (Washington: 1866), p. 6.
16. R. G. Pardee, *The Sabbath-School Index* (Philadelphia: J. C. Garrigues and Co., 1868), p. 19.
17. Charles I. Foster, *An Errand of Mercy* (Chapel Hill: The University of North Carolina Press, 1960), p. 166.
18. Sunday School Union of London *Proceedings,* Annual Meeting, (May 13, 1828).

CHAPTER II   *In Every Destitute Place*

1. American Sunday School Union, *Sixth Annual Report* (1830), p. 3.
2. American Sunday School Union, *Eighth Annual Report* (1832), p. 31.
3. *Ibid.*, p. 32. Italics added.
4. American Sunday School Union, *Eleventh Annual Report* (1835), p. 17.
5. Cited by Dorchester, *op. cit.,* p. 428.
6. Clifford S. Griffin, "Religious Benevolence as Social Control, 1815-1860," *The Mississippi Valley Historical Review* (XLIV, December, 1957), p. 434.
7. *Ibid.*, p. 432.
8. *Ibid.*, p. 430.
9. Letter from files of the St. Louis History Collection, Missouri State Historical Society. Italics added.
10. American Sunday School Union, *Thirtienth Annual Report* (1854), p. 77.
11. Joseph H. McCullagh, *The Sunday School Man of the South* (Philadelphia: American Sunday School Union, 1889), p. 81.
12. B. Paxson Drury, *A Fruitful Life* (Philadelphia: American Sunday School Union, 1882), p. 109.
13. Cited by L. Rudolph, *Hoosier Zion* (New Haven: Yale University Press, 1963), p. 165.
14. The American Sunday School Magazine (I, October, 1824), p. 1. Italics added.
15. *The Daisydingle Sunday-School* (Philadelphia: American Sunday School Union, n.d.), p. 14.
16. Carter Godwin Woodson, *The Education of the Negro Prior to 1861* (New York: G. P. Putnam's Sons, 1915), p. 153-54.

17. *Ibid.,* p. 163.
18. Charles C. Jones, *The Religious Instruction of the Negroes* (Savannah: Thomas Purse, 1842), p. 198.
19. Third International Sunday School Convention, Toronto (1881), p. 171.
20. Anson Phelps Stokes, *Church and State in the United States* (New York: Harper & Brothers, 1950), Vol. II, p. 191.

CHAPTER III   *From Death to Sunbeams*

1. Cited by Charles C. Cole, Jr., *The Social Ideas of the Northern Evangelists* (New York: Columbia University Press, 1954), p. 99.
2. Ford K. Brown, *op. cit.,* p. 457.
3. *A Memorial for Sunday School Boys* (Philadelphia: American Sunday School Union, n.d.), pp. 9-11.
4. Philippe Aries, *Centuries of Childhood* (New York: Vintage Books, 1962), pp. 38, 39.
5. Andrew H. Mills, "A Hundred Years of Sunday School History in Illinois, 1818-1918," *Transactions of the Illinois State Historical Society* (Publication 24 of the Illinois State Historical Library, 1918), p. 103.
6. Cited by Charles C. Cole, Jr., *op. cit.,* p. 99.
7. Perry Miller, *op. cit.,* p. 25.
8. John S. Hart, *The Sunday School Idea* (Philadelphia: J. C. Garrigues & Co., 1874), p. 151.
9. C. W. Wendte, "Sentiment and Song in the Sunday School," *Religious Education* (III), p. 95.
10. *An Easy Introduction to the Knowledge of Nature* (Philadelphia: American Sunday School Union, n.d.), pp. 79,82.
11. "A Father's Care," *Songs for Little Singers* (Philadelphia: Hall-Mack Company, 1914), p. 43.
12. "What are the Flowers Saying?" *Songs for Little Singers,* p. 22.
13. "God is Everywhere," *Songs for Little Singers,* p. 23.
14. "I Will be a Sunbeam," *Songs for Little Singers,* (ed.) J. Lincoln Hall and Elsie Duncan Yale (Philadelphia: Hall-Mack Company, 1909), p. 58.
15. Nellie Grahame, *The Cloud and the Sunbeam* (Philadelphia: Presbyterian Board of Publication, 1865), p. 25.
16. "Tell Him to Halt," *Hymnal for Primary Classes* (Philadelphia: American Sunday School Union, 1896), #86.
17. "The Best Use of a Penny," *Hymnal for Primary Classes,* #126.

CHAPTER IV   *A Pinch of Harvard, A Heap of Tammany Hall*

1. Andrew Mills, *op. cit.,* p. 104. Reynolds' remark about the Sunday school as the "cream" of the church was recorded in *Official Report of the Tenth International Sunday School Convention* (1902), p. 233.

2. Simeon Gilbert, *The Lesson System* (New York: Phillips and Hunt, 1879), p. 26.
3. H. Wayne Morgan, "Toward National Unity," *The Gilded Age,* revised edition (ed.) H. Wayne Morgan (Syracuse: Syracuse University Press, 1970), p. 2.
4. Henry F. May, *Protestant Churches and Industrial America* (New York: Harper & Row, 1967), p. 77.
5. Daniel J. Boorstin, *The Americans: The National Experience* (New York: Random House, 1965), p. 121.
6. Francis J. McConnell, *By The Way* (New York: Abingdon-Cokesbury Press, 1952), p. 233.
7. Gilbert, *op. cit.,* p. 37.
8. *Ibid.,* p. 46.
9. *Eighth International Sunday School Convention* (1896), p. 252.
10. *Official Report of the Tenth International Sunday School Convention* (1902), pp. 166, 167.
11. *Ninth International Sunday School Convention* (1899), p. 92.
12. *The Autobiography of William Allen White* (New York: The Macmillan Company, 1946), p. 44.
13. *First International Sunday School Convention* (1875), pp. 45, 47.
14. Shailer Mathews, *New Faith for Old* (New York: The Macmillan Company, 1936), p. 245.
15. *Sixth International Sunday School Convention* (1890), pp. 169-70.
16. Thomas Curtis Clark, "An Estimate of the International Sunday School Convention," *The Christian Century* (XXXI, July 9, 1914).
17. *Official Report of the Tenth International Sunday School Convention* (1902), p. 224.
18. *Seventh International Sunday School Convention* (1893), p. 178.
19. *Eighth International Sunday School Convention* (1896), p. 178.
20. *Ninth International Sunday School Convention* (1899), p. 35.
21. *Fifth International Sunday School Convention* (1887), p. 82.
22. Carter Godwin Woodson, *The History of the Negro Church* (Washington, D. C.: The Associated Publishers, 1921), p. 268. Italics added.
23. Mark Twain, *The Adventures of Tom Sawyer* (New York: Grosset and Dunlap, 1946), p. 39.
24. Raymond B. Fosdick, *John D. Rockefeller, Jr.: A Portrait* (New York: Harper & Brothers, 1956), pp. 126-27.

CHAPTER V   *Old-Time School vs. New-Time School*

1. Wesner Fallaw, "Now for the School of the Church!" *The Christian Century* (LXII, June 6, 1945), p. 676.
2. Clarence H. Benson, *A Popular History of Christian Education* (Chicago: Moody Press, 1943), p. 9.
3. George H. Betts, "If the Sunday School Fails," *The Christian Century* (XLII, January 29, 1925), p. 155.

4. Lockhart Amerman, "The Menace of the Sunday School," *The Christian Century* (LXI, February 9, 1944), p. 173.
5. Charles Clayton Morrison, "Protestantism and the Public School," *The Christian Century* (LXIII, April 17, 1946), p. 490.
6. Henry Seidel Canby, *American Memoir* (Boston: Houghton Mifflin Company, 1947), p. 68.
7. Willard Uphaus, *Commitment* (New York: McGraw-Hill Book Company, Inc., 1963), p. 28.
8. Franklin D. Elmer, "Recent Progress in the Sunday School," *Education and National Character* (Chicago: The Religious Education Association, 1908), p. 279.
9. Raymond B. Fosdick, *op. cit.,* p. 24.
10. Shailer Mathews, *op. cit.,* p. 249.
11. Robert and Helen S. Lynd, *Middletown* (New York: Harcourt, Brace and Co., 1929), pp. 391, 388-89.
12. Henry F. May, *The End of American Innocence* (Chicago: Quadrangle Books, 1964), p. 14. Italics added.
13. H. M. Hamill, "The Sunday-School as an Educational Force," *The Development of the Sunday School:* 1780-1905 (Boston: The Executive Committee of the International Sunday School Association, 1905), p. 177.
14. Richard Hofstadter, *The Paranoid Style in American Politics and other Essays* (New York: Alfred A. Knopf, 1966), p. 78.
15. "Look Dad, I'm Leaving," *Time* (LXXX, December 7, 1962), p. 52.
16. *Ibid.*
17. Elmer Towns, "How Are the 'Coon Dogs,'" *Christian Life* (XXXII, August, 1970), p. 42.
18. Elmer Towns, "America's Largest Sunday Schools are Growing," *Christian Life* (XXXII, August, 1970), p. 15.
19. James DeForest Murch, *Teach or Perish!* (Grand Rapids: William B. Eerdmans Publishing Company, 1961), p. 52.
20. Elmer Towns, "America's Largest Sunday Schools are Growing," *op. cit.,* pp. 16-17.
21. Peter Berger, *The Sacred Canopy* (Garden City: Doubleday & Company, Inc. 1967), p. 137.
22. Cited by J. Paul Williams, "When the Clergy Abdicates," *The Christian Century* (LXIII, January 16, 1946), p. 74.
23. Edward L. R. Elson, "J. Edgar Hoover—Churchman," *Presbyterian Life* (I, November 27, 1948), p. 5.
24. Wesley Shrader, "Our Troubled Sunday Schools," *Life* (XLII, February 11, 1957), p. 110.
25. Willie Morris, *North Toward Home* (Boston: Houghton Mifflin Company, 1967), p. 40.

Acknowledgments

This is the first volume to grow out of a study project on "The History of the World Sunday School Movement." The book would not have been possible apart from the imaginative foresight and generosity of several interested friends of the World Council of Christian Education (WCCE). In particular, we would like to pay tribute to Mr. Coleman Burke for his leadership, as well as to Dr. Ralph N. Mould, General Secretary of the WCCE. Both have been most helpful. Mr. Loren Walters and the New York Office of the WCCE have also assisted our work in various ways. Although the Council has been cooperative from the outset, it should not be held responsible for any of the particular judgments expressed in this book.

Likewise we are grateful to Dr. William B. Kennedy of the

World Council of Churches who, together with Professor Robert T. Handy of Union Theological Seminary, New York, encouraged us not to be satisfied with safe or easy answers to complex problems of historical interpretation. In the same vein the authors have been greatly helped by the advice of Professor C. Ellis Nelson of Union Theological Seminary, the Rev. Andrew Wright and Dr. J. Kenneth Meir of London, and Dr. Nelson Chappel of Toronto. Dr. Gerald E. Knoff of the National Council of Churches has graciously shared his insights. So has one of the veterans of Sunday school work—Dr. Luther A. Weigle, whose contributions to the movement have been immeasurable. We owe much to the findings and speculations of our associates in research: Mr. Robert Craig, who assisted in the whole enterprise; Mr. James Fraser, who investigated the beginnings of the American Sunday school; Mr. Robert Harsh, who gave help all along the way; Mrs. Alice Dickerson Hatt, who led us all in the rediscovery of the musical heritage of the Sunday school; and not least, Miss Emily Hewitt, whose explorations of the nineteenth-century literature were valuable and instructive. Professor Grant S. Shockley of Emory University took time from a busy schedule to develop the outlines of a history of the black Sunday school in America. Professor Charles Kniker of Iowa State University located some crucial material for our narrative.

The authors especially appreciated the spirited help of others during the hectic months of preparation: the encouragement of our wives, Katharine Lynn and Juanita Wright; the aid of Mrs. Jean Stetson of North Leeds, Maine; the support of the Auburn Program at Union Theological Seminary—Mrs. Rosalee Maxwell and Mrs. Shirley Skirvin, and particularly the editorial work of Mrs. Virginia Clifford.